PEARL HARBOR ATTACK

EDWIN P. HOYT

STERLING

New York / London
www.sterlingpublishing.com/kids

A FLYING POINT PRESS BOOK

Eyewitness accounts courtesy of the Pearl Harbor Survivors Association.

Design: PlutoMedia and John T. Perry III
Front cover painting: Don Kloetzke, courtesy of Thunder Mountain Press
(www.thunderart.com)
Frontispiece photograph: United States Naval Historical Center
Interior photographs: United States Naval Historical Center and Corbis

STERLING and the distinctive Sterling logo are registered trademarks of
Sterling Publishing Co., Inc.

Library of Congress Cataloging-in-Publication Data

Hoyt, Edwin Palmer.
Pearl Harbor attack / Edwin P. Hoyt. — Updated ed.
p. cm. — (Sterling Point books)
Revision of: Pearl Harbor. 2001.
Includes bibliographical references and index.
ISBN-13: 978-1-4027-5704-4
ISBN-10: 1-4027-5704-2
1. Pearl Harbor (Hawaii), Attack on, 1941. I. Hoyt, Edwin Palmer. Pearl Harbor. II. Title.

D767.92.H69 2008
940.54'26693--dc22   2007041161

2   4   6   8   10   9   7   5   3   1

Published by Sterling Publishing Co., Inc.
387 Park Avenue South, New York, NY 10016
Original edition published by Random House, Inc.
Copyright © 1991 by Edwin P. Hoyt
New material in this updated edition
Copyright © 2008 by Flying Point Press
Maps and diagrams copyright © Richard Thompson, Creative Freelancers, Inc.
Distributed in Canada by Sterling Publishing
c/o Canadian Manda Group, 165 Dufferin Street
Toronto, Ontario, Canada M6K 3H6
Distributed in the United Kingdom by GMC Distribution Services
Castle Place, 166 High Street, Lewes, East Sussex, England BN7 1XU
Distributed in Australia by Capricorn Link (Australia) Pty, Ltd.
P.O. Box 704, Windsor, NSW 2756, Australia

Printed in China
All rights reserved

Sterling ISBN-13: 978-1-4027-5704-4
ISBN-10: 1-4027-5704-2

For information about custom editions, special sales, premium and
corporate purchases, please contact Sterling Special Sales
Department at 800–505–5489 or specialsales@sterlingpublishing.com

If it is necessary to fight in the first six months to a year of a war against the United States and England I will run wild. But I must tell you if the war be prolonged for two or three years I have no confidence in our ultimate victory.

—Admiral Isoroku Yamamoto

TABLE OF CONTENTS

CONTENTS

JAPANESE

Admiral Isoroku Yamamoto: Commander in Chief of the Japanese Fleet. He attended Harvard University and was opposed to the war but conceived and directed the attack against Pearl Harbor.

Admiral Chuichi Nagumo: A senior admiral in the Imperial Japanese Navy. He opposed Yamamato's plan but was put in charge of the attack task force.

Rear Admiral Ryunosuke Kusaka: Chief of Staff of the First Air Fleet.

Lt. Commander Suguru Suzuki: The aviation officer aboard the spy ship, *Taiyo Maru,* who reported on the Pearl Harbor defenses to Japanese naval leaders just prior to the attack.

Commander Minoru Genda: A brilliant aviator, he developed plans and led the attack.

Commander Mitsuo Fuchida: Leader of the first-wave attackers, he lost only 29 planes out of 363 launched.

AMERICANS

Franklin D. Roosevelt: President of the United States.

Frank Knox: Secretary of the Navy. He believed that carrier-based aircraft could execute a surprise attack on Pearl Harbor.

Commander Husband E. Kimmel: Commander in Chief of the Pacific Fleet (CinCPAC). He did not believe Japan would venture so far from home to attack.

Admiral Harold R. Stark: Chief of Naval Operations. He believed an attack was improbable.

General Douglas MacArthur: Commander of U.S. Army Forces in the Far East.

Lt. General Walter Short: Chief United States Army Commander in Hawaii.

Admiral William F. Halsey: Commanded Task Force Eight comprised of the carrier *Enterprise,* three heavy cruisers, and nine destroyers. His task force was not in Pearl Harbor at the time of the attack.

General George Marshall: Army Chief of Staff.

Lt. William Outerbridge: Captain of the destroyer USS *Ward*.

THE ROOTS OF CONFLICT

THE REASONS FOR JAPAN'S ATTACK ON THE United States lie in that island nation's history.

Until the United States Navy under Commodore Matthew Perry sailed into Tokyo Bay in 1853 with a fleet of gunboats, Japan had been isolated from the rest of the world for 250 years. Japanese were forbidden on pain of death from having contact with *gaikokugin,* foreigners (literally people from the outside).

While Europe modernized and emerged from the Middle Ages, Japan remained a feudal country. The country's ruler was the *Shogun,* a military leader. The position was hereditary.

The Shoguns ruled through local lords, the *daimyos.*

The backbone of both the Shogun's and daimyos' power were the *samurai,* strong, brave, and unquestioningly loyal warriors. Death before dishonor was a key teaching of *Bushido,* the code of the samurai.

Japan also had an emperor. The Japanese revered their emperor and believed that he was descended from the Sun Goddess. However, under the Shoguns, the Emperors had no power and filled their days writing poetry or performing religious ceremonies.

The Japanese believed themselves to be superior to other people. No foreign conqueror had ever subjugated them. Two invasions by Kublai Khan, Emperor of China, in the 13th century had been beaten back. The Japanese believed that the gods themselves had protected Japan. Typhoons had destroyed the Chinese fleet on both occasions. The Japanese called these storms *kamikaze* (divine wind).

In the mid-19th century most Japanese and their leaders were happy with the society they had built in isolation from the rest of the world. The Japanese just wanted to be left alone.

Thus when Commodore Perry sailed into their waters with modern ships and weapons, the Japanese were shocked. Their leaders realized the inferiority of

Japanese weapons. They realized that Japan was in danger of sharing the fate of the rest of Asia, colonization.

A decade after Perry's arrival, samurai in southern Japan began a rebellion that overthrew the Shogun and restored the power of the Emperor. Japanese traveled to Europe and the U.S. to learn about Western technology, politics, and business. In the last half of the 19th century Japan rapidly industrialized. Japan's industrial revolution was crammed into 30 years, not the century plus that it took in Europe and America.

By the beginning of the early 20th century Japan was accepted as a junior partner by the Western colonial powers. Imitating Western nations, Japan acquired colonies of its own: Taiwan and Korea. Japanese troops joined French, British, German, Russian, and American soldiers in putting down the Boxer Rebellion in China. Japan also signed a naval treaty with Great Britain.

In 1904 Japanese and Russian interests in China collided. Japan decided that it had to resort to military force. Most Westerners felt that Japan would be crushed by the Russian colossus. Japan decided that national self-interest trumped a sense of fair play. Without warning the Japanese Navy attacked the Russian Far East Fleet. Japan won. Russia then sent its Baltic Fleet around the world to confront the victorious Japanese. Once again, to the world's surprise, Japan defeated the Russians. Japan had learned a lesson. You didn't have to play by the rules—as long as you won.

In 1914 Japan entered World War I on the side of the Allies. After the war Japan was awarded control over several Pacific Island groups. The Japanese believed that they were being accepted as a dominant power in the Pacific and the Far East. However, Japan still had not achieved its goal of full equality with the Western Powers.

In the early 1920s the great world powers agreed to limit the number of warships each country could build. Under the agreement the United States and Britain were allowed to build more ships than Japan. Japan had been accepted as a partner, but still a junior partner. Japan was resentful of these restrictions.

More importantly, in order to continue to develop its industries and to build powerful armies and navies, Japan needed access to raw materials such as oil, iron ore, rubber, and coal. Japan had few of these natural resources in the home islands. The Japanese leaders felt that Japan needed to control lands containing these resources. Otherwise Japan's future would always be subject to the decisions of foreigners. Japan felt that no country could be great if its well-being was subject to the whims of others.

Japan decided to get these needed resources the old-fashioned way—by colonization. In the 1930s Japan invaded Manchuria, a province in northern China, and later added China's capital, Beijing, and many Chinese seaports. There was strong negative reaction in Europe to Japan's use of force.

The Japanese felt that the rules were being changed in the middle of the game: it was okay for white Europe to have colonies, but it wasn't okay for non-white countries to have colonies. Japan had not realized that, in the wake of World War I, a change had occurred in Western opinion. Colonialism was seen as a relic of the 19th century, the "bad old days." Japan was not the only country to run afoul of the new rules. Italy, which invaded Ethiopia, was also ostracized for its attempt to acquire new colonies.

America's and Europe's concern about Japan increased when Japan allied itself with Nazi Germany and Fascist Italy in 1940.

President Roosevelt, who had long been concerned about Japanese plans in the Pacific, took action to curb the Japanese from making further advances. He clamped an embargo on Japan to cut off the supplies of oil, rubber, and steel that Japan needed to fuel its war machine. In addition, he moved the United States Navy's Pacific fleet from San Diego to Hawaii—much closer to Japan.

These moves, of course, only served to anger the Japanese and make them even more determined to achieve their goals of preeminence in the Pacific. The oil embargo particularly worried the Japanese leaders. Without oil Japan's industries as well as their army and navy would collapse. Japan's leaders felt that they had to act before time ran out. If they submitted without a fight, they would be sacrificing 70 years of modernization.

Despite Japan's obvious actions, there were few leaders in the United States who believed that a tiny nation like Japan would dare to make a surprise attack on the United States. They had not paid attention to the lesson of the Russo-Japanese War, which had started with a surprise attack by Japan.

Also, our leaders misunderstood the psyche and motives of the Japanese leaders. This lack of understanding was to soon have severe and tragic consequences for our soldiers and sailors in Hawaii and would vault the United States into World War II.

THE EDITORS

CHAPTER 1

A GOOD DAY FOR GOLF

AT 7:35 ON THE MORNING OF DECEMBER 7, 1941 families at the American Naval Base in Hawaii were just waking up. It was Sunday, the sky was bright and clear, and Admiral Husband Kimmel, Commander in Chief of the Pacific Fleet, was looking forward to a game of golf with General Walter Short.

Overhead the reconnaissance plane from the Japanese cruiser *Chikuma* was lazily circling Pearl Harbor. It radioed back to the Japanese fleet:

"Enemy formation at anchor: nine battleships, one heavy cruiser, six light cruisers are in the harbor." Then came a meteorological report: Wind direction from eighty degrees, speed fourteen meters, clearance over

1

enemy fleet one thousand seven hundred meters, cloud density seven. Then the *Chikuma* plane headed back to the fleet, its job done.

Meanwhile, a reconnaissance plane from the Japanese cruiser *Tone*, sent to Maui to examine the Lahaina anchorage, reported that the fleet was not in that area. The real object of their search was the three American aircraft carrier task forces, which were nowhere in evidence in the island, much to the disappointment of the Japanese. So they knew that whatever elements of the American fleet were missing from Pearl Harbor— the carriers, in particular—were not in the Hawaiian Islands this day, but where were they? The absence of the carriers and the inability of the Japanese to locate their areas of Operations were to have a major effect on the Japanese air strike.

At 7:55 on Ford Island, U.S. Navy Commander Logan Ramsay saw an airplane streak across the station, and prepared to report the incident as a breach of safety regulations—until he realized that the red he saw on the aircraft was not a squadron commander's insignia but a Japanese flag, and that the object he saw drop from the plane was not a black bag but a bomb.

Commander Ramsay ran to the radio room of the Ford Island command center and told the radiomen on duty to send a single message, in the clear, in plain English.

"Air raid, Pearl Harbor. This is not a drill . . ."

CHAPTER 2

JAPANESE STRATEGY AND
THE SPY SHIP

Military leaders in Japan disagreed about the best strategy for an attack on the American Navy at Pearl Harbor. Admiral Chuichi Nagumo, one of the most senior Japanese naval officers, favored a strategy centered on battleships; and Admiral Isoroku Yamamoto, Commander in Chief of the Japanese Fleet, believed that aircraft carriers had the best chance of success.

Battleship tradition had it that the battleship was the major fighting force of the fleet. The carrier, with its guns limited to anti-aircraft and its flat deck, seemed to be almost a liability at sea, vulnerable to submarine attack and easily sunk by a battleship. But of course as airmen understood, the secret of a carrier's defense was carried on the carrier— the antisubmarine aircraft patrols and the combat air patrols that circled the carrier when it was at sea.

On April 10, 1941, the Japanese did what Admiral Yamamoto and other airmen of the Imperial Navy had long advocated: They organized the First Air

Admiral Chuichi Nagumo, the commander of the First Air Fleet, the task force assigned to attack Pearl Harbor.

Fleet and Striking Force or *Kido Butai,* a change that would ultimately bring together the six carriers *Akagi, Kaga, Soryu, Hiryu, Shokaku,* and *Zuikaku,* all modern fast ships. Ironically, however, Admiral Nagumo, an opponent of the aircraft carrier strategy, was chosen as the commander of the First Air Fleet. His appointment caused much controversy because of his opposition to Yamamoto's plan. Many feared he would be unable to carry out a successful operation.

The First Air Fleet trained all spring in 1941, and by August it had achieved a high degree of skill in night as

Admiral Isoroku Yamamoto, the commander of the combined Japanese fleet. Yamamoto devised the strategy for the attack on Pearl Harbor.

well as daylight operations. Kagoshima, on the southern tip of Kyushu Island, became the training ground for the torpedo bombers because its layout was similar to Pearl Harbor, and day and night all summer, planes roared down above the city, so low that some citizens began to object, although it did them no good.

The fighter pilots were going to use the newest model Zero fighters, and they had to get used to them, to carrier landings, interception and dog fighting, two planes against three, two planes against four, two planes against six. Day after day the fighter pilots flew, until Lieutenant Commander Shigeru Itaya, their training officer, was satisfied that they were doing the job as he wanted it done.

The new carrier, *Shokaku,* 29,800 tons, left the Yokosuka Naval Dockyard on August 8, 1941, and took aboard her aircraft—twelve fighters, eighteen dive-bombers, and eighteen torpedo bombers. Her air units had already been formed and were training at Usa, Oita, and Omura air bases. So were the pilots and crew of *Zuikaku*, which was being hurried to completion for the Pearl Harbor attack. She was finished on September 25, and then the two new ships became the Fifth Carrier Division, the last two of the six carriers that would participate in the Pearl Harbor raid.

In August 1941, a new element was added to the Pearl Harbor raid. For some time the Japanese Navy had been experimenting with midget submarines that weighed 46 tons and carried two torpedoes and a crew of two men. They were 76 feet long and only 6 feet wide, a tight fit even for Japanese sailors. They had a top speed of 19 knots, but this speed used fuel at an alarming rate. At 4 knots they had a range of 100 miles. The submarine corps was eager to test the battle qualities of these midgets.

In September, in spite of Admiral Nagumo's reluctance, the Pearl Harbor plan began to come together. The key staff officers of the First Air Fleet were assembled by Chief of Staff Ryunosuke Kusaka and briefed officially for the first time on the mission they were going to perform.

In October, the bomber crews began to learn how to use torpedoes in very shallow water, similar to the waters of Pearl Harbor. They would climb to 2,000 meters and fly over the eastern tip of the volcano Sakurajima that stuck out in Kagoshima Bay, then down the valley of the Kotsuka River. The planes would be at 500-meter intervals. They would go down to 50 meters altitude, flying down the valley toward Kagoshima, and fly over the city at 40 meters. After they passed over the Yamagataya Department Store on the port side they would see a large water tank on the shore. As they passed over they would drop down to 20 meters and release a torpedo. The target would be 500 meters from the shore. After they released,

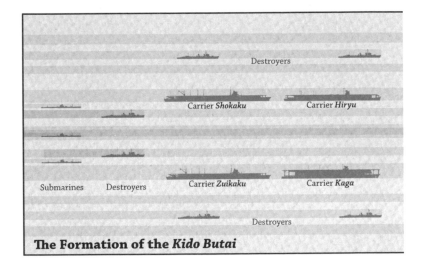

The Formation of the *Kido Butai*

at a speed of 160 knots, they would fly straight, then climb to starboard and return to base. They had to be very careful. At those altitudes even the slightest error could mean disaster.

The pilots of the Second Carrier Division trained at Kasanohara near Kanoya air base using the battleship *Settsu,* an ancient hulk moored in Ariake Bay as a target for the dive-bombers. They used bombs that emitted white smoke when they made a hit. After much practice the pilots decided it would be a fine idea to delay release of their bombs, not releasing them from 600 meters but instead at 450 meters. The chances of getting a hit would be increased, they said.

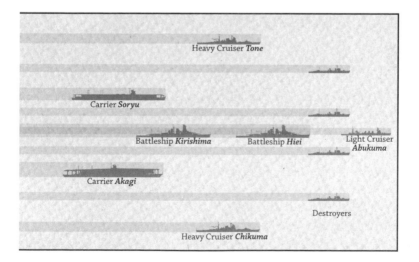

Heavy Cruiser *Tone*

Carrier *Soryu*

Battleship *Kirishima*   Battleship *Hiei*   Light Cruiser *Abukuma*

Carrier *Akagi*

Destroyers

Heavy Cruiser *Chikuma*

Meanwhile in early November, Japanese Naval Intelligence had sent the merchant ship *Taiyo Maru* sailing from Yokohama, ostensibly to pick up any Japanese citizens in Hawaii and on the west coast of America who wanted to return home in these difficult times between the nations. Actually the *Taiyo Maru* was on an espionage mission, carrying three naval officers—Commander Toshihide Maejima, Sublieutenant Keio Matsuo, both submariners who were to get information that would be valuable for the midget submarines, and Lt. Commander Suguru Suzuki, an aviation officer.

On the voyage to Hawaii, following the route the striking force would take, they made careful weather observations and kept careful records. They also watched constantly for ships to see if any American warships were moving about these waters. When the *Taiyo Maru* was 100 miles north of Oahu they did see a formation of American planes, and Suzuki noted that this could be the attack line, the point beyond which the Americans would not be patrolling.

When they got to Hawaii they summed up the results. The weather all the way across had been fine, except for one storm. They had sighted no patrol craft north of Midway, and reconnaissance north of Oahu could not extend more than 200 miles. They had not sighted a single vessel on the whole voyage.

The *Taiyo Maru* entered Honolulu Harbor on Saturday morning, November 1. They were coming in on the weekend, and could see what it would be like for Admiral Nagumo a few weeks in the future. These officers did not go ashore because they did not want to attract attention. Instead they set up a telephone line from the bridge of the ship to the gangway on the dock. Several members of the Japanese consulate staff came to the dock as was quite natural, and they conferred with the naval officers over this telephone. Consul Nagano Kita came aboard and conferred with Suzuki. They asked for and got all the information the consular staff had on the American fleet. They observed all the army and navy patrol flights that flew around Hawaii, types and number of aircraft, and their formations.

On November 5, the *Taiyo Maru* left Honolulu again and headed back to Japan. She was the last Japanese ship to call at that Hawaiian port.

As the Japanese ships began to assemble at Hitokappu Bay, the *Taiyo Maru* reached Japan having taken the route home that Admiral Nagumo would use. They saw that air patrols were weak in the north and west, that

11

there were no planes in the Midway skies, and they saw no ships on the voyage. When the ship reached Japan the naval officers were whisked off and driven swiftly to Tokyo. They were to report that afternoon to the Naval General Staff.

At two o'clock in the afternoon they went to a room in the Navy Ministry. Many important people were there from the staff and operations and from intelligence. Lieutenant Commander Suzuki reported first; the admirals were visibly impressed and relieved to hear that the American air patrols were weak. But one question Suzuki could not answer. What were the Americans doing with their carriers?

CHAPTER 3

WARNINGS IGNORED

IN THE MONTHS BEFORE THE ATTACK ON PEARL Harbor, few in Washington believed that the Japanese would really stage an air strike across the Pacific Ocean against this formidable naval base. The conventional wisdom said that an attack could not possibly occur because it could not possibly succeed. In the spring of 1941 a report from the United States Army claimed that Oahu was the "strongest fortress in the world."

This attitude was as widely held in Japan as it was in the United States and accounts for the fact that Admiral Yamamoto did not actually receive the go-ahead from Naval Headquarters in Tokyo until just a few days before launching the attack from the Kuril Islands.

One important aspect of the failure of the Americans to realize what was coming was the orientation of the defense community in Washington. Almost all eyes were turned to the Atlantic Ocean where the U-boat menace from Germany was very severe that fall of 1941.

Another part of the problem was the breakdown of the intelligence processes in Washington.

The fact was that over the summer months the Japanese had sent out many clues, which were either misinterpreted by the American intelligence community or ignored.

For more than ten years the Americans had been breaking the Japanese naval and diplomatic codes. The information had become scantier since 1940 when the Japanese changed several of their codes, and American code breakers were playing catch-up.

In May 1941, the head of the Office of Naval Intelligence noted that he thought that the Japanese would move very soon against the United States. When Admiral Kelly Turner, the naval chief of war plans, saw the note, he scribbled on it: "I don't think the Japs are going to jump, now or ever."

The Pacific Fleet command struggled valiantly to put together the shreds of intelligence it could get. For example, in the first week of November they were able to deduce that the Japanese fleet was preparing for some sort of major action from the nature and extent of the radio traffic.

But a little information can be a dangerous thing: In mid-November, when there were no transmissions from the aircraft carriers, the Pacific command deduced that they were in port replenishing. They could not have been more wrong. The carriers were on their way to the Kuril Islands, and from now on carrier radio silence would be maintained until the Pearl Harbor attack.

Commander Minoru Genda, the brilliant air tactician who devised the specific attack plan. Genda is shown here in a photograph taken when he was visiting the United States before the war.

Later in November, the radio traffic intercepted at Pearl Harbor indicated that the Japanese objectives would be Malaysia, the Dutch East Indies, and the Philippines. Even Washington was suddenly and belatedly aware of the danger. No one, Admiral Stark

Admiral Husband E. Kimmel, Commander of the United States Pacific fleet. Kimmel was blamed for not being ready for the attack on Pearl Harbor.

told Admiral Kimmel in a letter that week, would be surprised at a Japanese surprise attack.

But, of course, he did not mean on Hawaii.

On December 1st in Washington the navy cryptographers deciphered a Japanese message from Tokyo to the Japanese ambassador in Berlin, Germany, assuring the Germans that war was about to break out between Japan and the Western powers. Had Admiral Kimmel been sent this message he might have known what was going to happen. Later, Kimmel would be blamed, and same say scapegoated, for not being ready for the attack.

On December 2nd there was still no information about the Japanese aircraft carriers, and this worried Admiral Kimmel. He asked his intelligence officer, Commander Edwin Layton, if the Japanese carriers might not at that

16

moment be rounding Diamond Head and was told that they might well be for all Layton knew.

On December 4th Pacific fleet headquarters learned that the Japanese consulate was burning its codes and records.

By December 6th all information at Pearl Harbor indicated war was coming immediately, but war in the South China Sea, not war at Pearl Harbor.

CHAPTER 4

COUNTDOWN

ON THE MORNING OF DECEMBER 6, 1941, Lieutenant William Outerbridge took the destroyer *Ward* to sea for his first cruise. They would be out for three days, and then would come back into port for one day, and then go out for three more days.

It was a beautiful day to be sailing out of Pearl Harbor, the breeze was light and warm, and when they got to sea, it was a question of drifting across the buoys and listening for propeller noises, easy duty it seemed.

Lieutenant Outerbridge was very favorably impressed with his crew, the young men full of zeal and enthusiasm. The officers all seemed to know their jobs and did them competently and with grace. He gave silent thanks to his predecessor for the training of the crew.

The *Ward's* job in the Inshore Patrol was to watch over a square 3 miles to each side, just off the entrance to Pearl Harbor, the big American naval base in the Hawaiian Islands, base of the U.S. Pacific Fleet.

The night of December 6, the army air force headquarters on Hawaii had word that a B-17 flight was on its way from California. Twelve new B-17 bombers were being ferried to the Philippines to shore up the defense force there; it was a long flight and they planned to re-fuel at Hickam Field near Pearl Harbor.

In such cases it was the air force habit to ask Radio Station KGMB to stay on the air all night long, so the pilots of the bombers could home in on the radio signal. This night was no exception, and KGMB was asked to broadcast all night and complied as it always had, for it was up late in this Christmas season. The Japanese at sea, as well as the American pilots, had the pleasant sound of the big band music to lull them that night.

As the Americans of the fleet were sleeping, the Japanese of the submarine force that had approached Oahu in the last few days were moving into action. The Japanese

Japanese plane leaves aircraft carrier Shokaku
to attack Pearl Harbor.

submarine I-16 released the 20-foot midget submarine
that it carried on its deck. An hour later, nine miles off the
entrance to the Pearl Harbor channel, the I-22 sent its
two-man submarine on its way. The target: the ships
inside Pearl Harbor, which were to be attacked today in
the opening move of the Pacific War.

At 2:15 A.M., the I-18, which was sitting 12 miles off
Pearl Harbor, let go her two-man midget submarine. Just

before three o'clock the I-20 launched its two-man midget, and half an hour later the I-24 launched the fifth midget submarine.

Meanwhile, to the north of Oahu Island, the Japanese task force was preparing to launch the aircraft that would attack the American fleet in conjunction with the midget torpedo attacks. The midget submarines, of course, were to provide a diversion if possible. Admiral Isoroku Yamamoto, Commander of the Japanese Combined Fleet and the father of the Pearl Harbor attack plan, regarded the midget submarine operation as sort of a stunt, but he could not deny that the midgets might have some value, and now was the time to test it.

Aboard the Japanese carriers, preflight operations had begun at midnight—the aircraft were being brought up from the hangar decks of the carriers and spotted for takeoff.

At 3:58 in the morning of December 7th, the watch aboard the *Ward* had a flashing light signal from the American minesweeper *Condor:*

We have sighted a suspicious object, which looks like a submarine. It appears to be standing to the westward from our present position.

The signalman aboard the *Ward* acknowledged the signal and Skipper Outerbridge was notified. He ordered General Quarters. *(General Quarters is a condition of readiness when naval action is imminent. All battle stations are fully manned and alert; ammunition is ready for instant loading; guns may be loaded.)* The ship got up speed to 20 knots and closed with the *Condor,* asking for additional information. The ships exchanged several messages over voice radio. After reaching the position of the *Condor,* the *Ward* turned west, toward Barber's Point, and searched. The search revealed nothing. After half an hour or so, Lieutenant Outerbridge decided that if it had been a submarine, it had evaded them. He told the watch to secure the ship from General Quarters, and told the executive officer, who was on duty, to let the men sleep in the next morning since they had been up so late this night. Then Skipper Outerbridge went back to bed in his sea cabin.

Coming down from the north Pacific, the Japanese of the carrier striking force were up at four o'clock in the morning and getting ready for the attack, with a breakfast of snapper and rice. The Japanese force was about 325 miles north of Oahu. In the radio room the operators were still listening to the lilting music of Honolulu radio station KGMB, whose uninterrupted broadcast showed that the Americans suspected nothing.

By 5:00 A.M. all the pilots were up and dressed. Commander Mitsuo Fuchida, the leader of the air strike, ate breakfast and went to the briefing room underneath the flight deck to confer with the leaders of the torpedo bombers, dive-bombers, and fighter group that would accompany his twin-engine high level bombers in the attack. The seas were roughing up and this would necessitate extreme caution in takeoff to prevent accidents.

The aircrews assembled in their ready rooms for the final briefing, and then the pilots got ready to man their planes. Just before six o'clock the carriers turned into the wind and the launching of the planes began. Commander Fuchida was given a headband by the crew of *Akagi,* and he tied it around his helmet before he slipped into the cockpit of his plane.

The Zero fighters took off first. One fighter pilot miscalculated and crashed into the sea on takeoff, but the pilot was picked up by a destroyer. Another Zero began to cough, and the pilot had to pull out of the formation and wait for permission to land and abort for engine trouble. But those were the only losses. As soon as the attacking fighters were launched, so was the combat air patrol that would protect the carrier fleet from any surprises from the Americans.

Next the high level bombers went off, with Commander Fuchida's plane going first. Each bomber carried a pilot, a bombardier observer, and a radio operator. Each crewman had a pistol, a map of Oahu, and survival gear in case he had to land in the sea.

After the high level bombers got off the decks of the six carriers, the torpedo bombers began to take off, each with its own three-man crew, too. Then the dive-bombers began to launch, and soon there were 183 planes in the air, the first wave of the attack against Pearl Harbor: forty-three fighters, forty-nine high level bombers, forty torpedo planes, and fifty-one dive-bombers.

For fifteen minutes the aircraft circled the ship formation and formed up into their flight pattern, checking to be sure there would be no more aborts. At 6:20 A.M. Commander Fuchida led his high level bombers across the bow of the *Akagi,* and everyone knew that was the signal. The other planes formed up and followed, and the attack unit moved off in the direction of the target: PEARL HARBOR.

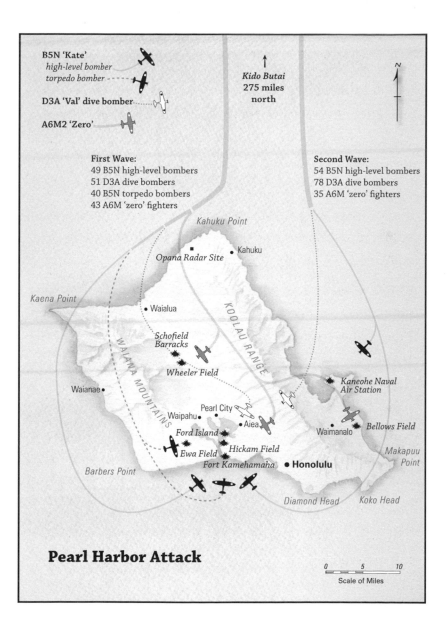

B5N 'Kate'
high-level bomber
torpedo bomber
D3A 'Val' dive bomber
A6M2 'Zero'

Kido Butai
275 miles
north

N

First Wave:
49 B5N high-level bombers
51 D3A dive bombers
40 B5N torpedo bombers
43 A6M 'zero' fighters

Second Wave:
54 B5N high-level bombers
78 D3A dive bombers
35 A6M 'zero' fighters

Kahuku Point
Opana Radar Site
Kahuku

Kaena Point
Waialua

KOOLAU RANGE

Schofield
Barracks

WAIANAE MOUNTAINS

Wheeler Field

Waianae

Kaneohe Naval
Air Station

Waipahu
Pearl City
Aiea
Ford Island
Ewa Field
Hickam Field
Fort Kamehamaha

Waimanalo
Bellows Field

Makapuu
Point

Barbers Point

Fort Kamehamaha
● Honolulu

Diamond Head
Koko Head

Pearl Harbor Attack

0   5   10
Scale of Miles

As soon as the last plane left the decks of the carriers, Admiral Nagumo ordered the fleet to turn south at 20 knots, to be closer to Oahu when the time came to recover the aircraft. On the hangar decks of the carriers, the plane handlers worked furiously to prepare the second strike.

The pilots and aircrews assembled in the ready rooms and prepared to go. Commander Genda, the genius who had planned the whole attack, gave some last minute instructions. He told Lieutenant Chihaya, the commander of the *Akagi's* second dive-bomber echelon, to check on the enemy anti-aircraft fire. Genda was thinking about a third strike that day, and if the anti-aircraft fire was too strong, he would not employ any torpedo planes on the third strike. The decision whether or not to launch a third strike would have important consequences for the course of the war.

CHAPTER 5

AIR RAID PEARL HARBOR

AT 6:30 ON THE MORNING OF DECEMBER 7TH, the air attack force was still an hour and a half away from Hawaii. The captain of the American ship *Antares* was preparing to enter Pearl Harbor when he saw what he thought was the conning tower of a small submarine. At the same time the object was seen by the helmsman of the destroyer USS *Ward*.

Lieutenant William Outerbridge was still snoring in his sea cabin when he was rudely awakened by Lieutenant Goepner. Once was enough, Skipper Outerbridge thought, for a really inconsequential matter like the report on the *Antares*. Twice was too much.

"Captain, come onto the bridge," said Lieutenant Goepner.

"Now look here, Goepner," the skipper protested. "That's stern talk for the Officer of the Deck to be giving. You know it means I have got to come to the bridge. I've only been here one day, but I want you to realize that giving commands like that is serious business. I fully expect to find something up there."

"Captain, come to the bridge" was the imperious answer. So Lieutenant Outerbridge got up to the bridge on the double, sensing that something was not right.

Goepner pointed. "We've been watching that object. It appears to be following the *Antares*. It looks like a buoy, but it's moving and we think it is a submarine."

Outerbridge took a hard look.

"I believe that's a submarine," he said. "Go to General Quarters."

Goepner sounded the gong and the crew came to General Quarters at 6:35.

"If that is a submarine," said Outerbridge, "we will attack."

"I'll go to my battle station," said Goepner. He was the gunnery officer.

"Yes, Doughty will take the deck."

Lieutenant Goepner ordered the guns all loaded. The depth charges were all set for "ready." The destroyer was an old four-stack World War I model, and she had only two boilers fired up and could only make about 20 knots. So at 20 knots they went after the submarine.

As they approached, Captain Outerbridge wondered whether he should shoot or ram. Since he did not know how big the submarine was, he decided not to ram, because they had the speed up to 24 knots and the ramming might knock the bottom out of the destroyer.

So he decided to shoot and drop depth charges.

At about 75 yards off, he ordered the gunners to open fire. Gun No. 1 fired first, and missed. Gun No. 3 fired next, and the shell hit the submarine at the base of the conning tower; there was a feather of water, and the shell appeared to penetrate. Some of the men said they saw a hole in the submarine. They passed by the submarine so close that other men said they thought the destroyer was going to ram. They dropped four depth charges, the charges exploded, and the submarine sank.

After the submarine sank they looked around and saw a white sampan that was in the restricted area where it had no right to be. They decided to investigate it. But on the way, they sent a message to Pearl Harbor saying that they had attacked a submarine, and a second message saying that they had attacked with guns, which meant a surfaced submarine.

The *Ward* then chased the sampan, which hove to. They went alongside and the sampan captain, a Japanese, came out of the cabin waving a white flag, which they thought was odd. They sent for the Coast Guard, which sent a cutter from Honolulu Harbor, which then escorted the sampan into Honolulu Harbor.

At about the same time Fourteenth Naval District also had a report from Patrol Wing 2 that a patrol plane had depth bombed and sunk a small submarine off the entrance to Pearl Harbor. So two of the Japanese miniature submarines were accounted for, but no one had yet really sounded an alert at Pearl Harbor!

Shortly after 7:00 A.M. the Japanese carriers turned east into the wind again, and increased speed to 24 knots. The second strike began to launch. The sky was quite cloudy, with visibility of 12 miles and ceiling around 5,000 feet. The thirty-five fighters took off first—no aborts this time. In this second wave came fifty-four horizontal bombers, which would strike the American airfields: Hickam, Kaneohe Naval Air Station, and Ford

Island. The seventy-eight dive-bombers in this wave would strike the ships in Pearl Harbor a second time. One dive-bomber did not make it, the engine ran rough, and the flight was scratched. But all the other aircraft got off safely and began winging their way toward Oahu to follow on the heels of the first wave. A total of 351 Japanese planes were going in to attack.

Admiral Nagumo and Admiral Kusaka stood on the bridge of the *Akagi* and watched as the planes disappeared into the murk ahead. Commander Genda watched for a little while and then went to the control room to await the signal from Fuchida that the air attack was beginning.

In Washington that morning, General Marshall arrived at his office to learn that big events were brewing in Asia. The navy had the same information, from code breaks. In the months leading up to December 7th, the Japanese and American governments had serious disagreements about military matters in Asia. Talks between the countries had been getting increasingly heated. That morning a Japanese message of ultimatum arrived. General Marshall sent an alert message to Hawaii:

Japanese are presenting at 1:00 P.M. Eastern Standard Time today what amounts to an ultimatum. Also they are under orders to destroy their code machine immediately. Just what significance the hour set may have we do not know, but be on the alert, accordingly. Inform naval authorities of this communication. Marshall.

There were problems, atmospheric and other, with army communications that day, so the army sent the message by Western Union, the commercial telegraph and cable company. The message did not have a priority designation. When it reached Hawaii, it was pigeonholed for routine delivery to Fort Shafter. It sat as the minutes ticked away.

At sea, about 250 miles west of Hawaii, Admiral William F. Halsey's Task Force 8, built around the carrier *Enterprise,* was heading back to Pearl Harbor after delivering its load of aircraft to Wake Island. The admiral was still expecting trouble, so he sent off a search patrol that dawn to look for Japanese carriers. On the hangar and flight deck, the dive-bomber squadron was getting ready to fly off and make the trip to Hawaii as the carrier steamed home.

On the northern tip of Oahu the two soldiers manning the Opana Mobile Radar station had been there since they went on duty at 4:00 A.M. Private Joseph L. Lockard was senior, and the junior member of the team was Private George E. Elliott. At 7:00 A.M. they were scheduled to shut down operations and go off duty. They got ready to leave when suddenly Lockard saw a mess of dots on their screen, so many that it was hard to think of them as

Admiral William F. Halsey, Jr., Commander of Task Force 8 in 1941. His ships, consisting primarily of aircraft carriers, were about 250 miles from Pearl Harbor at the time of the Japanese attack. These were the ships that the Japanese did not find at Pearl Harbor. Halsey would later go on to command U.S. naval forces in the south Pacific.

blips. He watched for a couple of minutes and counted more than fifty images, at first 132 miles from Oahu. Elliott suggested that they telephone the combat information center, but Lockard said it might be an aberration of the machine. But Elliott persisted, so Lockard agreed to telephone, on the basis that it would be good exercise for the information center to deal with an unexpected report. The call was made and consumed about five minutes, during which time the blips moved 25 miles nearer to Oahu.

Theoretically the information center was manned by a group of plotters who moved markers around a big table, symbolizing the movement of aircraft. Above them at the second-floor level was a large balcony where the controller and pursuit officer sat and watched. It was their job to order planes up to intercept enemy planes or supposed enemy planes, but this morning nothing was expected except one flight of B-17s en route from California to the Philippines. The controller had left early and so had all the plotters. The switchboard operator, Private Joseph McDonald, thought he was the only one on duty, but as he took this call from Elliott at the radar station he saw Lieutenant Kermit Tyler, a brand-new pursuit officer who had served only one day previously on the job.

When Private Elliott said what he thought the radarmen were seeing, Private McDonald was impressed enough to ask Lieutenant Tyler to pick up the phone. Private Lockard got on the other end and told what they had seen—the biggest sighting he had ever seen—and gave the course and speed. Tyler was impressed. It might be a big group of planes from one of the carriers. Then he remembered that KGMB had been on the air all night and that he had heard that when B-17s were coming in the radio station stayed on all night, so he attributed the number of blips to the B-17s that were supposed to be arriving. Lockard did not tell him that he had seen more than fifty blips. That news might have alerted Lieutenant Tyler that there were too many blips. The coming of the B-17s was a matter of security not to be shared with privates like Lockard, so not knowing how many blips there were, Lieutenant Tyler said not to worry about the sighting and hung up the phone.

At this time, when the radarmen were watching the Japanese attack coming in without knowing what they were seeing, the destroyer *Ward* had established another submarine contact out by the entrance to Pearl Harbor. She dropped more depth charges and saw a black oil bubble about 300 yards astern. Skipper Outerbridge believed he had gotten to another submarine.

On the northern tip of Oahu, the radarmen stayed on duty, fascinated with the sight of these blips coming in so steadily. From 7:20 to 7:39, when they lost the blips due to radar distortion by the mountains, they tracked the incoming flight.

Four minutes before contact was lost, the reconnaissance plane from the cruiser *Chikuma*, which was lazily circling over Pearl Harbor, radioed back to the Japanese fleet:

"Enemy formation at anchor; nine battleships, one heavy cruiser, six light cruisers are in the harbor." Then came a meteorological report: "Wind direction from eighty degrees, speed fourteen meters, clearance over enemy fleet one thousand seven hundred meters, cloud density seven." Then the Chikuma *plane headed back to the fleet, its job done.*

In Hawaii the army was not talking to the navy and the navy was not talking to the army. The navy submarine alert was not communicated to army headquarters, where it might at least have triggered enough response to force the army air force to move its aircraft from their wingtip-to-wingtip positions on the fields.

Nor did the navy learn anything about the "more than fifty blips" coming in from the north, which would at least have told them where the Japanese carriers were located. Each service was serene in its ignorance of what was happening and not at all concerned about the moments ahead. At Fourteenth Naval District headquarters, Admiral Claude C. Bloch was inclined to believe that the sightings by the *Ward* were just the result of too much enthusiasm.

So when the Pacific Fleet duty officer telephoned Admiral Kimmel, the Admiral had no knowledge that in Washington the Secretaries of State, War, and Navy were waiting anxiously for a statement expected momentarily from the Japanese that they thought would forecast war, that General Marshall had sent a war warning that was still resting in a cubbyhole in the telegraph office, or that the radarmen at Opana Point on North Oahu were watching a whole armada of blips closing on Oahu. The duty officer reported the activities of the *Ward*. Standing alone, they seemed odd but no cause for alarm. Had they been added to all the other factors, all separated and unknown to the command, they would have raised the hackles on the back of Admiral Kimmel's neck. Just now he was wondering how long it would take him to dispose of this problem so that he could get down to the serious business of his regular Sunday morning golf game with General Short.

CHAPTER 6

FIRST WAVE ATTACK

LT. COMMANDER SHIGERU ITAYA LED HIS
Zero fighters in, and remembered clearly what he saw:

Pearl Harbor was still asleep in the morning mist. It was calm and serene inside the harbor, not even a trace of smoke from the ships at Oahu. The orderly groups of barracks, the wriggling white line of the automobile road climbing up to the mountaintop; fine objectives of attack in all directions. In line with these, inside the harbor, were important ships of the Pacific Fleet, strung out and anchored two ships side by side in an orderly manner.

Aboard those ships the men of the Pacific Fleet were following their Sunday morning routine. As always in this period when watchfulness had been ordained for months, the fleet never completely relaxed, but in harbor on the weekends went to Condition 3 of readiness, which meant minimal manning. The morning watch, which would go off duty at 8:00 A.M., was tidying up after the night, wiping down the barrels of the guns and shining the brass. In the wardrooms, the officers who had the day watch were just finishing their breakfasts and the petty officers and the men were doing the same in their mess rooms. Of all the war ships in the harbor that morning— seventy fighting ships and twenty-four auxiliaries of various sorts—only one, the destroyer *Helm,* was underway.

After the yeoman in the Fourteenth Naval District radio room got his message from the *Ward* straight and decoded, he gave it to Lt. Commander Harold Kaminsky, the senior duty officer of the Fourteenth District. But that had not been until 7:12, and Kaminsky had been on the telephone since, trying to raise people. Admiral Bloch, Kaminsky's commander, had gotten through to the operations office, and the ready-duty destroyer *Monaghan* had been ordered to get underway, but she had not yet, and the standby destroyer was just getting up steam. There was action at Pearl Harbor by this time, but it was unseen.

From Honolulu came the sound of church bells, pealing for the congregation to come to the eight o'clock Mass for the Roman Catholics and eight o'clock Communion for the Protestants.

Lieutenant Graham D. Bonnell of the supply corps was aboard the USS *San Francisco,* which was undergoing an overhaul at the Pearl Harbor Navy Yard. Her engines had been torn down, there was no fuel aboard, the turrets were inoperative, and there was no ammunition aboard. That morning Lieutenant Bonnell was awake at around 7:30. He lay semiconscious for a few minutes, and then suddenly he was jerked awake by the sound of a screaming dive of an airplane. He looked out the porthole in the direction of Ford Island and saw a plane diving on one of the hangars. He saw the red balls on the airplane, but it did not register at the moment.

"I lay back on the bunk and thought to myself: Navy dive-bombers are the best in the world."
At about that time he heard a loud explosion and

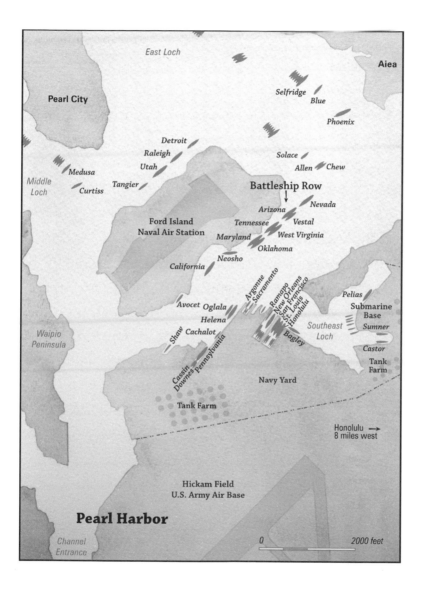

East Loch

Aiea

Pearl City

Selfridge / Blue

Phoenix

Detroit /
Raleigh /
Utah /

Solace /

Allen / Chew

Middle
Loch

Medusa
Curtiss

Tangier /

Battleship Row
↓

Arizona / Nevada

Ford Island
Naval Air Station

Tennessee / Vestal
Maryland / West Virginia

Oklahoma

Neosho

California /

Argonne
Sacramento
Ramapo
New Orleans
San Francisco
St. Louis
Honolulu

Pelias /

Submarine
Base

Avocet / Oglala
Helena
Shaw Cachalot /

Southeast
Loch

Sumner

Bagley

Castor

Waipio
Peninsula

Tank
Farm

Cassin
Downes Pennsylvania

Navy Yard

Honolulu →
8 miles west

Tank Farm

Hickam Field
U.S. Army Air Base

Pearl Harbor

Channel
Entrance

0   2000 feet

jumped out of his bunk again in time to see the hangar on Ford Island go up in smoke.

By that time the general alarm aboard the ship was sounding. . . .

Lt. Commander Kaminsky had tried unsuccessfully to reach many people that morning, including Commander Vincent Murphy, the assistant war plans officer, who was duty officer at CinCPAC (Commander in Chief of the U.S. Pacific Fleet) headquarters that weekend. He finally did get through to Lt. Commander R. B. Black, the assistant duty officer. Black found Murphy at his quarters, dressing for the day. Commander Murphy instructed Black to be sure that Kaminsky had called Admiral Bloch, commander of the Fourteenth Naval District. Kaminsky's line was busy; he was trying to call other people. Black got back to Murphy, who said he would try Kaminsky and did, again without result. By the time Murphy got to his office the phone was ringing, and this time it was Lt. Commander Logan Ramsey of Patrol Wing 2, who reported that one of his planes had just sunk a submarine one mile off the entrance to Pearl Harbor. He told Ramsey that he had the same sort of report from a destroyer. They agreed that there was something funny going on.

Japanese aerial photograph of Battleship Row under attack.

Ramsey had just hung up the telephone when it rang again; it was Kaminsky. He reported on the *Ward* action, and then Murphy called Admiral Kimmel, who had been up for half an hour, getting ready for the golf game with General Short. He also reported on the sampan. Kimmel wondered how much credence to put on the reports. So did Admiral Bloch, when he got the report that morning.

Murphy called Kimmel back when he had further details of the stopping of the sampan. Murphy had just said those words when a yeoman rushed into his office.

"There's a message from the signal tower saying that

the Japanese are attacking Pearl Harbor and this is no drill," he shouted.

Murphy passed the word to the admiral, who slammed down the telephone and rushed outside his house, buttoning his white uniform jacket as he went.

Aboard the *Ward*, Lieutenant Outerbridge was excited by a new submarine contact near the Pearl Harbor entrance; they dropped more depth charges and reported again to Fourteenth Naval District. Executive Officer Doughty came to the bridge and asked if it would be possible to secure from General Quarters, because the men had been on full alert for a long time. It was just a few minutes before eight o'clock.

They heard several explosions. Doughty said he thought they were coming from the beach.

"That's probably that superhighway that's being built between Pearl Harbor and Honolulu, they're probably blasting this morning," said Outerbridge.

"No. It's not. Look over there. There are some planes coming straight down. It looks like they are bombing the place."

Outerbridge took a good look at the naval base. "My gosh," he said. "They are!"

Lt. Commander Ramsey was standing in the Ford

The destroyer USS Shaw *explodes during the Japanese attack. Despite suffering extensive damage, the* Shaw *was back in service by June 1942.*

Island Command Center, watching the color guard prepare to hoist the flag for the day. It was 7:55. He heard the scream of an airplane over the station and turned to a junior officer. "Get that fellow's name," he said. "I want to report him for about sixteen violations of the course and safety regulations." They watched the plane come down.

"Did you get his number?" asked Ramsey.

"No, but I think it must have been a squadron commander. I saw a band of red on the plane."

"Check all the squadrons and find out who is in the air," Ramsey demanded.

"I think I saw something black fall out of that plane."

Then an explosion emphasized the statement, and Ramsey knew what was happening. It was a Japanese plane and a Japanese bomb.

Rear Admiral William Rhea Furlong, commander of the service vessels of battle force, was strolling on the quarterdeck of his flagship, the minelayer *Oglala,* awaiting the word from the mess man that his breakfast was ready. The *Oglala* was sitting in the usual berth of the battleship *Pennsylvania,* which was in dry dock, nestled up against the cruiser *Helena.*

Furlong absentmindedly watched the planes come down, thinking of other matters, until he saw a bomb fall. What a stupid mistake for some pilot to be making; even a practice bomb could hurt somebody if it hit. But then the bomb hit and exploded, which no practice bomb should do. He also saw the red meatballs on the wings of the plane as it turned in the air. "Japanese," he shouted. "Man your stations!"

Lieutenant Bonnell's battle station was in the communications room in the superstructure of the *San Francisco.* He dressed in a hurry and headed for his battle station. The gun crews were organized and sent to other ships to help fight, since the *San Francisco* was as helpless as a hulk. . . .

Aboard the *Oglala* Admiral Furlong's men hoisted the flag: "All Ships in Harbor Sortie. . . ."

Lt. Commander Ramsey ran across the corridor from the command center at Ford Island to the radio room, and ordered all radiomen on duty to send out a message in plain English.

From the radio tower of the headquarters on Ford Island a message was sent out over the airwaves, a message that shook Americans in Washington and Manila.

"Air raid. Pearl Harbor. This is no drill."

The destroyer *Helm* was just entering West Loch, and she headed for the channel entrance. Her anti-aircraft guns were firing, and she brought down a plane. As she passed through the submarine gate, her crewmen spotted the Japanese submarine grounded on Tripod Reef and fired at the midget sub.

Aboard the battleship *West Virginia,* Ensign Roland S. Brooks saw what he thought was an internal explosion aboard the battleship *California,* and gave the order from the bridge: "Away fire and rescue party." This command brought men swarming up topside from below decks of the battleship, although he soon saw that the fire and smoke came not from the *California* but from the burning aircraft hangar on Ford Island.

Up above Pearl Harbor in the cane and pineapple fields, the rows of parked fighters at Wheeler Field stood wingtip to wingtip, with guards protecting them from sabotage on the ground, but nothing protecting them from the dive-bombers and fighters that swept down and smashed them. On Ford Island, the hangars were burning, and the bombs were raining down. About half the carrier-type planes on Ford Island and most of the hangars were gone or burning, and so were many patrol planes, the bombs sending pieces of PBY planes (amphibious patrol bombers) high in the air, to smash back into the concrete or splash in the water.

At Hickam Field Colonel William E. Farthing, the field commander, was in the tower talking with the adjutant of what was still called the Hawaiian Air Force. They were waiting for the arrival of the B-17 flight from California, which was supposed to come in very soon that morning. Suddenly a large group of aircraft appeared from the north, and dive-bombers peeled off and began bombing the aircraft and facilities at Hickam.

A fighter screeched down the streets of the officers' quarters, its guns spitting. Hangar No. 9 was the first to go, its roof shattered by bombers. The repair hangar was blasted. The enlisted men's hall took a direct hit, killing many men. The chapel was hit. A bomb released the prisoners from the guardhouse and another hit the firehouse and smashed the water mains.

The bombers then concentrated on the B-17 bombers, parked wingtip to wingtip, but the B-17s were tough and at the end of the attack four of them were still in flyable condition, although they had been repeatedly bombed and strafed in those first minutes. Half of Hickam's planes had been destroyed and the base facilities were hit very hard.

At Wheeler Field, where the dive-bombers had already set many planes afire, the Zeroes came back to strafe after hitting Hickam, and did more damage. There was no return fire from anti-aircraft guns, and they saw no American planes rising to meet them. The surprise was complete and a little awesome to the Japanese fliers. If the American pilots or gunners had wanted to fight, they could not have, because at night all the machine gun belts had been taken out of the planes and put into the hangars for safekeeping.

Wheeler Field that day housed ninety-one fighter planes, fifty-two modern P-40s, and thirty-nine older P-36s. Half the planes were destroyed, including thirty of the P-40s. At the marine airfield at Ewa, which had been strafed by fighters earlier, the returning dive-bombers destroyed nine of the eleven Wildcat fighters, eighteen of the thirty-two scout bombers, and six of eight utility planes.

So there were no American planes in the air to challenge the first wave of torpedo bombers as they swooped down on the ships in Pearl Harbor.

CHAPTER 7

BATTLESHIP ROW BOMBED!

ADMIRAL KIMMEL HAD DASHED OUT OF HIS house on Makalapa Drive and onto the lawn of his neighbor, Captain John B. Earle, chief of staff to Admiral Bloch. He stood there with Mrs. Earle watching the events down below at battleship row. First they saw the dive-bombers flying over Ford Island and Hickam, making figure-8 patterns as they bombed and then strafed. They could see the rising sun insignia on the planes' wings very clearly.

Lieutenant Shigeharu Murata was the first to drop. Here was the proof or failure of all the work that had been done over all the months to modify the Japanese aerial torpedoes to run in shallow water. Would they

USS Maryland *with USS* Oklahoma *capsized alongside.*

work? Murata dropped his torpedo and saw it crash against a battleship.

"*Atarimashita,*" shouted the observer. "It hit!"

Those words were transmitted back to the flagship, where they allayed the many fears of Admiral Nagumo that the torpedo attack would be a fiasco. Commander Genda smiled broadly. His efforts had been crowned with success.

The *West Virginia* was the first ship to be hit; she took

two torpedoes in rapid succession. The torpedoes knocked out all power, light, and communications. She listed, the list was corrected by flooding, and then she sank until the port bilge hit bottom and did not capsize. She was showered by debris from hits on other ships. *West Virginia* lost 2 officers and 103 men killed.

The *Oklahoma* was moored at Berth F-5 outboard of the battleship *Maryland*. A torpedo bomber came down to 60 feet above the water and put a torpedo into her. The pilot noticed that he was lower than the crow's nest of the battleship, and he zoomed above the deck. Then two other torpedo bombers loosed their torpedoes at the *Oklahoma*. The ship began to list. Soon the ship's executive officer, Commander J. L. Kenworthy, ordered abandon ship, and told the men to climb over the starboard side, for fear the battleship would capsize in the next few minutes.

A torpedo swept under the repair ship *Vestal* and hit the *Arizona*, but the real damage was done seconds later by a bomber, which dropped a bomb on the *Arizona*. The bomb hit beside the second turret, penetrated the forecastle, exploded in the forward magazine before it could be flooded, and wrecked the whole front end of the ship. Flames shot 500 feet in the air. Rear Admiral Isaac C.

Kidd and Captain Franklin van Valkenburgh were killed on the bridge. All this before 7:56, as Admiral Kimmel watched. Then a second bomb went down the stack, a third hit the boat deck, a fourth hit No. 4 turret, and four more hit in the superstructure. *Arizona* sank so fast that she did not capsize, and more than a thousand men were trapped below deck, either burned to death or drowned: The ship lost four-fifths of her ship's complement.

The battleship *Tennessee* was moored inboard of the West *Virginia,* and so she was protected from torpedoes by the other ship. But she took two bombs, one on the center of Gun Turret No. 2 and the other on Gun Turret No. 3. But most of the damage to this ship was caused by flaming debris from the *Arizona,* which was 75 feet astern of the *Tennessee.* Five men were killed or missing, and one officer and twenty men were wounded.

The battleship *Nevada* was moored astern of the *Arizona.* She had no ship tied up next to her. Her anti-aircraft guns opened fire quickly and accurately. Her guns shot down at least one of the torpedo bombers. Fifty-caliber machine guns shot down another. Because of the shooting she suffered only one torpedo hit and that was forward; the 45-foot-long hole flooded many compartments but left the power plant intact. She managed to get underway, and that is what she was doing at the time of the end of the first attack.

The *Maryland* and the *Oklahoma* were moored forward of the *Tennessee* and the *West Virginia,* and as noted the *Oklahoma* was hit early in the battle by three torpedoes. As the men were abandoning ship over the starboard side, two more torpedoes hit. The men were struggling to escape when the ship began to capsize. She rolled over and her masts stuck in the mud of the bottom. She lay with the starboard side of her bottom above water and part of the keel clear. Twenty officers and three hundred ninety-five men were killed or missing, and two officers and thirty men were wounded.

The *Maryland* was lucky. She was protected from the torpedoes by the *Oklahoma.* Her gunners shot down one torpedo plane before the pilot could launch his torpedo. She took only two bombs.

The *California,* the flagship of the cruiser squadron of the fleet, was hit by two torpedoes below the armor belt. She began to list to port and counter flooding was tried, but salt water got into the fuel tanks and she lost light and power, although she did not capsize. She was in trouble by the end of the first attack.

The last group of torpedo planes came in on the far

side of Ford Island where the seaplane tender *Tangier,* the target ship *Utah,* and the cruisers *Raleigh* and *Detroit* were moored. The *Tangier* was unhurt in this attack, the old battleship *Utah* was torpedoed twice by planes that thought she was a working battleship, and she capsized as Japanese planes returned to strafe.

The *Raleigh* was torpedoed, and the *Detroit* was near-missed by a torpedo in this first attack.

On the opposite side of the main channel, against battleship row, the minelayer *Oglala* was moored outboard of the light cruiser *Helena*. A torpedo plane, having missed the battleships, flew over and dropped its fish, which passed beneath the *Oglala* and smashed into the *Helena,* flooding an engine room. The anti-aircraft gunners gave such a good account of themselves that the dive-bombers veered away from the *Helena* and sought other targets. But the *Oglala* was also damaged by that torpedo blast, and as the captain was deciding to abandon ship because she was sinking, a bomb fell between the two ships and caused total loss of power on the *Oglala.*

In the dry dock the *Pennsylvania,* flagship of the Pacific Fleet, and two destroyers, the *Cassin* and *Downes,* were captives, but their anti-aircraft guns could be manned and they fought back against the dive-bombers that tried to attack them.

Kimmel watched from the Earle lawn in fascinated silence as the bombers hit battleship row. His car came up manned by his usual driver, and he dived into it. As it roared off down the hill Captain Freeland Daubin, commander of Submarine Squadron Four, jumped onto the runningboard and caught a ride. They reached the headquarters building down the hill just as the *California* was torpedoed in this first attack.

CHAPTER 8

EYEWITNESS ACCOUNTS FROM THE *ARIZONA* AND THE *OKLAHOMA*

Aboard the USS *Arizona*
George D. Phraner—Aviation Machinists Mate
  1st Class
Battle Station: Forward 5-inch Gun
19 years old

AS USUAL, THERE WAS A WARM BREEZE THAT Sunday morning. We had just finished breakfast and drifted out of the compartment to get a little air. This was our normal routine on weekends, as we had no workstation to report to. It was fortunate for us that we were

The wrecked superstructure of the USS Arizona burning at Pearl Harbor after the attack. Over 1,100 men were lost when the Arizona was sunk.

able to sleep in until 6:30 as many of us had been out the night before. Just as we left the mess area we heard this noise. We went outside to take a look because it's usually very quiet. When we arrived we could hear and see there were airplanes. I looked across the bow of the ship and could see large plumes of smoke coming up from Ford Island. At first, we didn't realize it was a bombing. It didn't mean anything to us until a large group of planes came near the ship and we could see for the first time the rising sun emblem on the plane wings. The bombing was becoming heavier all around us and we knew this was REALLY IT!

At first there was a rush of fear, the blood started to flow real fast. It was then that General Quarters sounded over the speaker and everything became automatic. My battle station was on a forward 5-inch gun and it was standard practice to keep only a limited amount of ammunition at the guns. There was only one ready gun crew on each side and mine wasn't one of them. There we were, the Japanese dropping bombs over us and we had no ammo. All the training and practicing for a year and when the real thing came we had no ammunition where we needed it. As unfortunate as this was, that simple fact was to save my life. Somehow the gun captain pointed at me and said, "You go aft and start bringing up the ammunition out of the magazines." The aft magazines were five decks below.

A few moments later I found myself deep below the water line in a part of the ship I normally would never be in. I remember getting these cases of ammo powder and shells weighing about 90 pounds each. I had begun lifting shells into the hoist when a deafening roar filled the room and the entire ship shuddered. It was the forward magazine. One and half million pounds of gunpowder

An aerial photograph of the Battleship Row area of Pearl Harbor after the attack. Note the damaged and overturned battleships and the trails of fuel oil leaking from the sunk and damaged ships.

exploding in a massive fireball disintegrating the whole forward part of the ship. Only moments before I stood with my gun crew just a few feet from the center of the explosion. Admiral Kidd, Captain Van Valkenburg, my whole gun crew was killed. Everyone on top.

Seconds after the explosion the lights went out and it was pitch black. Almost immediately a thick acrid smoke filled the magazine locker and the metal walls began to get hot. In the dark and not being able to breathe, we made our way to the door hatch, only to find it shut and locked. Somehow we were able to open the hatch and start to make our way up the ladder. I was nauseated by the smell of burning flesh, which turned out to be my own as I climbed up the hot ladder. A quick glance around revealed nothing in the darkness, but the moaning and sounds of falling bodies told me that some of my shipmates had succumbed to defeat and had died in their attempt to survive.

Getting through that choking kind of smoke was a real ordeal, the kind of smoke that really hurts your lungs. After a while I began to get weak and lightheaded. I could feel myself losing the battle to save my own life. I hung to the ladder, feeling good. I felt that it was all right for me to let go. At that moment I looked up and could see a small point of light through the smoke. It gave me the strength to go on. After what seemed to me like an eternity, I reached the deck gasping and choking. I lay down for a few moments. The warm Hawaiian air filled my lungs and cleared my head. I glanced over to the forward end of the ship to see nothing but a giant wall of flame and smoke. . . .

The sound of someone shouting "put out the fire" cut

through the sound of the battle, but it was obvious the ship was doomed. I made my way to the side of the ship, which by this time was sinking fast, and jumped off the fantail. The shoreline of Ford Island was only a short distance. There was burning oil all around the ship, but the aft was clear. After swimming to shore, I was taken to the naval air station. Every table in the mess hall had a man on it. After the attack was over, many of the battleship sailors, myself included, were taken to the USS *Tennessee*. I was there for one week and then transferred to the USS *Lexington* and an appointment with a place called the Coral Sea.

Aboard the USS *Oklahoma*
Adolph D. Mortensen—U.S. Navy Junior Officer
Battle Station: Boiler Room
25 years old

On Dec. 7, 1941, I was the junior officer of the boiler division of the battleship *Oklahoma*. Following late night duty, I had gone to sleep shortly after 4:00 A.M., that Sunday morning. Less than three hours later, the sound of a voice on the ship's loudspeaker, unmistakably different from the usual announcements, brought me quickly awake. "Air raid! Air raid! This is a real attack, real planes, real bombs!" followed by an obscenity, crackled from the loudspeaker. Wearing only a pajama trouser, I raced for my battle station in a boiler room, as the big ship leaped under my feet from explosions of torpedoes hitting deep in the hull. There were no lights. There was no chance of starting the engines. The order to abandon ship was passed along by voice as the ship began to list steeply.

I attempted to get to a compartment with large portholes through which I might escape when the veteran battleship turned turtle and I was propelled into the medical dispensary, its tiled floor now the sloping ceiling. I found myself with four other men in the dispensary with a small pocket of air trapped above the water, our only source for life.

With my feet, I found a porthole below the water. I was able to duck down in the water and turn the knobs on the port by hand. It was an eleven-inch porthole. The first two men got out quickly. The steward was hesitant and I pushed his head through and he pulled himself out. The ship's carpenter, Mr. Austin, a large man weighing over 200 pounds, knew he'd never make it through the porthole. He reached down and held the porthole open for me. I tried to take a deep breath, but the oxygen supply was about gone. As I went out, I scraped my hips squeezing through. I think that is where I lost my pajamas. Mr. Austin couldn't get out. His was the most noble and heroic act a man could perform, knowing full well that his minutes were few.

I swam the 15 to 20 feet to the oil-covered surface of the harbor. Then, I swam to ropes hanging from the ship's bottom that was still above water. Burning oil nearby sent pillars of smoke skyward. There was a deadly silence over the harbor, interspersed with violent explosions and bursts of gunfire.

As far as I can tell, I was the last man to escape from the ship without help. Cutting torches were used to try to free some of those trapped. I got away with nothing but my skin.

CHAPTER 9

CONTROL OF THE SKY

AFTER LIEUTENANT OUTERBRIDGE REALIZED that Pearl Harbor was under attack he doubled his vigilance. The *Ward* brought two more boilers into use and then had full power available as the ship steamed around the entrance to Pearl Harbor searching for more submarine contacts.

The *Monaghan,* the ready-duty destroyer, had been notified of the attacks around the entrance to the harbor a few minutes before the air attacks began, and she came out at 8:27. Steaming toward the harbor entrance, off Ford Island, she noticed that the tender *Curtiss* was flying a flag indicating the presence of an enemy submarine.

Japanese midget submarine on a beach in Oahu after the attack on Pearl Harbor.

The lookouts checked and saw a midget submarine in the harbor, under fire from the ships *Medusa* and *Curtiss*. The submarine launched a torpedo at the *Curtiss,* which missed and hit a dock at Pearl City. The *Monaghan* then took the submarine under fire with her guns. The first shot was over the submarine, and hit a barge. The destroyer prepared to ram the submarine, which then fired another torpedo. The torpedo missed and exploded against the shore.

The *Monaghan* then rammed the midget submarine,

passed over it as it sank, depth-charged it, and destroyed it. Her way from the ramming was so great that she collided with the barge that her first shot had hit, and had to back away. After firing a shot at a "submarine contact" that turned out to be a harbor buoy, the *Monaghan* then stood out into the channel and passed outside the harbor to join *Ward* in patrolling.

The destroyer *Helm,* meanwhile, was steaming in West Loch when her lookout spotted another Japanese midget submarine on Tripod Reef and fired at her. This was Ensign Sakamaki's submarine, and as the destroyer fired, the crewmen managed to get the midget sub off the reef and into the water. The *Helm* missed with her shots, and the midget began maneuvering again, but this time she got hopelessly lost and headed up around toward the north shore of the island, directly away from Pearl Harbor.

At 8:30 A.M. Hawaii time, 1:30 P.M. Eastern Standard Time, word of the attack ("This is not a drill") reached Washington. At first no one, including President Roosevelt, could believe that there had been an attack. Secretary of the Navy Frank Knox said he thought it must mean the Philippines but was assured that it was Pearl Harbor. Within a few minutes local radio stations all across America began to break into their quiet Sunday programs to announce that Pearl Harbor was even then under attack by Japanese aircraft.

In moments Secretary Knox was on the telephone to Admiral Bloch, receiving an eyewitness account of the aerial attack. Just then the stragglers from the first wave of Japanese attackers were heading back north and the second wave of the attack was coming in.

So, at that moment, were two flights of American aircraft—the B-17s from the West Coast and a group of planes from Admiral Halsey's carrier *Enterprise* that were coming in to land at Ford Island—on their way to Pearl Harbor.

The B-17s were very low on fuel and they headed for Hickam Field, to be told that the field was under attack and they could not land. The pilots then put down at airfields all over the island; one even landed on the navy golf course.

Eighteen Dauntless dive-bombers had taken off from the *Enterprise* early that morning and were coming in to what they thought was a landing at Ford Island. Instead they moved into a hail of fire from the second wave of attacking Japanese planes. One American dive-bomber was shot down by American anti-aircraft guns, and four were lost to Zero fighters.

Wrecked B-17 bomber at Hickam Field after the attack.

After the success of the first strike against the airfields the Japanese had complete control of the sky. After that first attack, not a single American navy plane rose into the air from Oahu to fight the Japanese. There was virtually nothing left to fly on the navy fields and at Hickam and Wheeler air bases. A handful of army fighters did get aloft from Bellows Field, a few miles south of Kaneohe, which had been hit in these first few minutes by one solitary strafer. The attack was so insignificant that a soldier crossing the barracks area on his way to church saw the

Japanese plane and heard the firing and thought it was an American training plane practicing gunnery with blank cartridges. He did not even turn off his path to the church.

But that single strafer alerted Colonel Leonard D. Weddington, commander of the field. He called together ground crews, and they first dispersed the planes, and then began to get them into action. The field had not been bothered by the Japanese because it was the home of a single observation squadron, and so they concentrated their efforts on the big fields. Since the field was not really damaged by the Japanese, they got their planes in the air and began attacking the Japanese. Luckily a squadron of P-40s had been attached to that field for a month of gunnery practice. The fighters took off—the only organized resistance on Oahu that morning. In all they claimed eleven enemy planes. But in fact they did not even slow the second wave of Japanese bombers as they came in to their designated targets.

By this time Admiral Kimmel had reached his office in the submarine base, and he stood at the window and watched the disaster that was continuing. A spent .50-caliber bullet broke through the glass and struck his jacket, raising a welt on his chest. It would have been better if it had killed him, the admiral said to his communications officer, who was standing next to him.

Outside, the second wave of Japanese dive-bombers that reached Pearl Harbor were concentrating on the battleship *Nevada,* which was underway and moving, although she was listing heavily. Tugs came out to help her and see that she did not block the channel. They managed to get the *Nevada* to Waipo Point, where she was beached.

In going after the *Nevada,* the Japanese bombers neglected the *Pennsylvania,* which, sitting in dry dock, was an easy target. One bomber did put a bomb into the *Pennsylvania*'s boat deck. Another bomber blew the bow off the destroyer *Shaw,* which was also in dry dock. The dry dock was flooded to prevent further damage from fire, but the fires were already creeping toward the magazines of the destroyers *Downes* and *Cassin,* which were also docked, and ten minutes after this strike, the two blew up. By nine o'clock that morning all of battleship row and all of Ford Island lay under a heavy curtain of smoke. The pilots of the Japanese planes could no longer see down through the murk, so they turned their attention to the northern side of Ford Island. The old battleship *Utah* got more attention and the three light cruisers nearby were all damaged.

Wrecks of destroyers USS Downes *and* Cassin *with* USS Pennsylvania *in the background. All three ships were in a drydock for repairs.*

Not long after Admiral Kimmel arrived at his head-quarters the Pacific Fleet staff began to assemble. One of those to arrive by car from Honolulu, where he lived, was

73

Commander Edwin Layton, the fleet intelligence officer. He checked in and was given first a list of the sunk and damaged ships, which appalled him so much he found it hard to concentrate. But he knew that his first task was to discover the whereabouts of the enemy fleet, because Admiral Kimmel would want to begin retaliating. Captain McMorris, the plans officer, called him into his plans office where several officers were sitting, stunned. Under cover of the racket from the two destroyers in the dry dock, which blew up, Commander Layton escaped to his own office, where he tried to find out the source of the Japanese planes that were surging over Pearl Harbor.

Layton had a call from the radio intelligence office, called Hypo. The duty officer told him they had gotten a direction finder bearing on the Japanese force. But the reading was bilateral. The Japanese were either due north or due south of Pearl Harbor, they could not tell which without another fix. Why could they not get a more accurate fix from the 75-foot antenna on a mountain north of Pearl Harbor? Layton wanted to know.

Because the telephone lines were down.

Why were the lines down?

Layton did not learn until later that it was because the

army had pulled the plug on the phone lines when the attack began, without warning to the navy. Neither had the army ever relayed the bearings of that force spotted at Opana Point. So the navy got no information or help at all from the army.

Layton was down in the fleet operations room, laying out the opposite bearings, when Admiral Kimmel came in.

"Where is the enemy?" the admiral asked.

"Either due north of us or due south, sir," said Commander Layton.

"Well, dammit, which?"

"I can't tell you, sir. It could be either one."

The tension was relieved by a report that Japanese parachutists were landing on Oahu. One report placed the enemy troops at Barber's Point. But all that was found there was a lone mechanic, picking up his parachute. He had been testing a plane when it was shot down by a Zero and he had parachuted to safety in blue coveralls with a red bandanna in the pocket. The report was of Japanese paratroops in blue overalls with red emblems.

A little later, Commander Layton had a call from Commander Joseph Rochefort, the head of radio intelligence. He could not help with the location, but he said he did know that the flagship of the Japanese force was the carrier *Akagi*.

How did he know? Demanded Layton.

Because the radiomen knew the "fist" or sending technique of the *Akagi* radio operator, and it was he who had been sending signals to the aircraft attacking the base.

That information was of no use to Admiral Kimmel, who wanted to make some decisions. He consulted with Captain McMorris, who was sure the Japanese ships had come up from the south and were lying south of Oahu. Kimmel ordered Admiral Halsey, who was not far away, to begin a search. Halsey was hampered because most of his dive-bombers were either in Oahu, shot down by the Zeroes, or on their way, but he began to search in the area indicated. All that he found there was water. Four of the B-17s soon managed to get off from Hickam air base and they went south to search. They found the cruiser *Minneapolis*. She sent a message: "No carriers in sight."

The message was garbled in transmission and arrived at Pearl Harbor as "Two carriers in sight," so Halsey was sent off again on a wild goose chase.

Admiral Wilson Brown's task force was also south of Oahu, and that afternoon as it steamed north, it was spotted by a PBY patrol plane returning from Midway.

Thinking this was the Japanese task force, the PBY bombed and hit one of Admiral Brown's cruisers to add to the damage and confusion of the day.

When the first wave of Japanese attacked Pearl Harbor, the second wave was about halfway between the carrier force and the American base, fifty-four high-altitude bombers at 11,500 feet, split into three groups, one bound for Hickam Field to complete the destruction of the air facilities there, and two other groups bound for the Kaneohe Naval Air Station and Ford Island, the little airfield of the carrier planes.

At 10,000 feet were the dive-bombers—seventy-eight of them in all—organized into four groups. Their primary task would be to find ships in the harbor and wreck as many of them as possible. Above the bombers flew thirty-five Zero fighters whose job was to protect the bombers, intercept American fighters, and strafe the airfields at Wheeler Field and the seaplane harbor and flying boat ramps of the Kaneohe air station.

Just at about the time that Commander Layton was worrying about the source of the Japanese attacks, the second wave struck.

One group of planes this time devoted its efforts to Bellows Field, where one of the incoming B-17s from the

West Coast had landed. Nine planes strafed the B-17 that had already been wrecked in crash-landing. Two of the American fighters were shot down as they tried to take off.

The high-level bombers concentrated on the hangars and shore installations at Kaneohe and wrecked a number of PBYs inside the hangars. One Zero fighter, strafing, was hit by a Browning automatic machine gun, and crashed into a road near the married officers' quarters. One more Zero was destroyed, but by the time the Japanese finished with Kaneohe, it was a real wreck. Three patrol bombers that were off on patrol escaped unharmed, six of those on the ground or in the water were damaged, and twenty-seven were destroyed. For the moment, at least, Kaneohe was out of commission.

At Wheeler Field some of the American fighters had begun to get into the air. Zeroes knocked two of them down as they were taking off. Lieutenant Kenneth Taylor shot down one or two Japanese planes, and Lieutenant George S. Welch shot one Zero off Taylor's tail. Then that particular group of Japanese fighters who were attacking Wheeler turned around and headed back for the rendezvous point to return to their carrier.

Sixteen other fighters headed for Hickam to strafe and protect fifty-four horizontal bombers heading that way. The leader of these fighters made one low-level pass over Hickam Field, and then climbed high, for this pilot's second duty was to assess the damage done to the American base and report to Commander Genda as the second strike was in progress so Genda could make some decisions about a third strike.

This fighter commander reported that heavy damage had been inflicted and gave no details.

The Japanese high-level bombers came in. The pilots of these planes were not as experienced as the bomber pilots of the first wave, but they did their job well, nonetheless. They also faced much more anti-aircraft fire than the first wave had received, and many of the planes were well sprinkled with flak holes as they flew in to bomb.

At Hickam Field, they scored direct hits on Hangar 13, Hangar 15, and the mess hall, where they killed all the Chinese cooks who had taken shelter there.

The dive-bombers faced very heavy anti-aircraft fire and so reported back to the *Akagi*. Commander Genda decided right then that if he was to call for a third strike, the torpedo bombers would stay aboard the carriers. The Pearl Harbor defenses were becoming stronger all the time.

By the time the dive-bombers reached Pearl Harbor the clouds of smoke from battleship row obscured much of the base. Down below the battleship *Nevada*, with a huge hole in her bow, moved past the overturned *Oklahoma*. The water was filled with oil and debris. The bombers singled out the *Nevada* and five bombs hit her. Before she could be beached the fore part of the ship was wrecked. Her casualties were 3 officers and 47 men killed and 5 officers and 104 men injured.

At ten o'clock the *Oglala*, which had been hard hit in the first raid, capsized and sank. The repair ship *Vestal* was moved to Aiea and beached. The destroyer *Blue* got underway and started out of the harbor. Her anti-aircraft gunners were firing and brought down at least one Japanese plane.

Looking for targets, the dive-bombers found the cruiser *Raleigh*, which had been torpedoed in the first attack, and they dropped a bomb on her and then one pilot strafed the ship. One bomber dropped a bomb that struck the pier about 15 feet from the cruiser *Honolulu* and did some damage. That same bomb did some damage to the cruiser *St. Louis,* which was moored near the *Honolulu,* but the *St. Louis* got up steam and got underway.

By this time the Japanese bombers had run out of bombs and had gone back to strafe the airfields again. The last of the midget submarines then got into action, firing two torpedoes at the *St. Louis,* both of which missed, and the submarine popped to the surface. The gunners of *St. Louis* were firing at the submarine and thought they sank it.

As the Japanese moved, so did Lieutenants Welch and Taylor, who had landed at Wheeler Field and re-gassed and rearmed their planes in a respite between attacks. Over Barber's Point, the two American pilots ran into some Japanese planes and began shooting. In the end they were credited with seven enemy planes destroyed, four from the first raid and three from the second.

Some of the Japanese bombers and fighters came down over Hickam Field once they had exhausted all their bombs and continued to strafe, mostly aiming for the B-17s, several of which they damaged further.

But the second wave was more expensive for the Japanese, because the Americans were finally getting their defenses up, and the raid cost the enemy six fighter planes and fourteen dive-bombers.

Up above the mess of Pearl Harbor, Commander Fuchida's bomber was still circling, now badly damaged by anti-aircraft fire. He assessed the damage done to the Americans: eight battleships, three light cruisers, three destroyers, and four auxiliary ships either sunk or damaged. Eighteen vessels in all knocked out of action by this attack. The U.S. Navy had also lost thirteen fighters, twenty-one scout bombers, forty-six patrol bombers, three utility planes, two transports, and two training planes, besides the five *Enterprise* carrier planes shot down by American guns and the enemy.

The army air force had taken a very bad pasting, with four B-17s lost, twelve B-18 bombers lost, two A-20 bombers, thirty-two P-40s, twenty P-36s, four P-26s, and two OA-9 aircraft. Damaged planes numbered eighty-eight pursuit planes, six reconnaissance aircraft, and thirty-four bombers.

American casualties were high: 2,400 navy, army, marines, and civilians killed, and 1,178 wounded. All this had been done at a cost to the Japanese of twenty-nine planes, one large submarine, and five midget submarines, with all their crews except Ensign Sakamaki, who washed up on the north shore of Oahu that day and became a prisoner of war.

CHAPTER 10

EYEWITNESS ACCOUNTS FROM HICKAM AIR FIELD AND THE *PENNSYLVANIA*

Tech. Sgt Pesek Runs for His Life at Hickam Field
Joseph A. Pesek
Technical Sergeant, United States Army Air Corps,
   5th Bomber Group.
23 years old

ON THE MORNING OF DECEMBER 7, 1941, I got up shortly after 6 A.M. and walked to the NCO club for breakfast, which was adjacent to the Pearl Harbor Naval Base. At the time I was a Tech Sergeant in the 5th Bomber Group and sharing half of a duplex government house with Joe Barrett, 4th Recon Squadron. After breakfast, I headed for the bus stop to wait for the 8:05 bus to take me to Honolulu where I was to play golf at the Wai Lai Golf Course.

While sitting there on a bench, I noticed a large flight of aircraft approaching from the northwest flying at an altitude of about 15,000 feet and at a distance that made identification impossible. I had seen similar flights come in preceding the arrival of U.S. aircraft carriers and just assumed another of our carriers was coming into port at Pearl Harbor. They approached at a point almost due north of where I was sitting and suddenly began to peel off in steep dives into the harbor. I watched a large torpedo-shaped bomb drop from the first plane followed by a huge explosion.

At the time, I thought it strange but possible that the Navy was conducting some sort of exercise and possibly destroying something over in the west locks where the target ship *Utah* and other old ships were moored. As the first plane pulled up only several hundred feet to my left with machine guns blazing, I saw the rising sun insignia on the wings and knew we were under attack.

He was flying over Hickam Air Field at an altitude of approximately 150 ft. A young boy was waiting at the bus stop with me and I told him to get home as fast as he could. By that time, clouds of black smoke were rising over the Harbor and planes were pulling up across Hickam toward the flight line with machine guns firing. When I got back to my quarters, Joe Barrett was just getting up to see what all the noise was about. I yelled to him to move it as we were under attack.

After throwing on a pair of coveralls over my civies, we took off running toward the consolidated barracks and flight line. By this time, things were hectic and we had to hit the ground every few minutes due to low-flying strafing planes. As we were crossing the parade ground headed for the hangar line, we ran into Dave Jacobson and three other guys trying to set up an old WWI water-cooled machine gun and they were having problems with the tripod.

Joe and I both had prior hitches in the Infantry so we had it assembled and in operational order quickly. I believe that had there not been a lull in the strafing, we would have stayed right there, but I guess it was not to be.

As we ran toward the hangar, we stayed close to the barracks so we wouldn't be out in the open as the planes were again overhead. . . . When we got to the hangar, Joe went to his plane and I went into Hangar 7. They were passing out rifles from the armament room so I got in line thinking at least it may be some protection later on. By the time I reached the head of the line, all rifles and helmets had been given out. I then started to carry canisters of 50-caliber ammo out of the armament room so they could be loaded into any of the aircraft still in commission. Several minutes later, I was returning for another canister when someone coming out said all the ammo was out, so I turned around and headed out the large sliding doors. Just then the hangar took a hit from a large bomb dropped from a high-altitude flight. It felt as though the whole hangar was lifted from the ground. The next thing I knew, I was picking myself up off the ramp between hangars 7 and 11, my back covered with white plaster blown out from the hangar.

Someone ran up to me and handed me a pint of whiskey. I took a gulp holding the bottle with both hands and although I don't remember being scared, my hands shook so much I almost dropped the bottle before giving it back. Next, I went to the adjacent Hangar 9 where Ed Caton, Freddie Lewis, and J. P. Bock were. For a little while, there was another lull so we just sat and talked. I remember J.P. smoking a cigarette so fast it was like a fuse burning with a flame at the end of it. In about 15 minutes, the planes were back and Ed and Freddie were kneeling on the flight line side of the hangar, firing at them as they flew along the row of hangars. Once they passed, I took off across the runway toward the John Rogers Airport, which was located where the present Honolulu International Airport is now. Before I got to the middle of the runway, I saw low-flying aircraft approaching from the east and I hit the ground again. While waiting for them to pass, someone hit the ground next to me and said, "Where are you headed, soldier?" I looked up and it was Brig. Gen. Jacob H. Rudolph, commander of the Eighteenth Bombardment Wing. I said, "I'm not sure where I'm going, but I know it's away from the hangars."

I got up and started to run again and almost made the edge of the runway when three more planes came at me. They were so low that I could see the ground kicking up where their machine-gun bullets were hitting. I hit the ground again covering my head with my hands. It seemed as though a thousand things passed through my mind, mostly of home and my family. I could not believe it when those three planes passed right over without hitting me.

I looked up as they passed and thought the sky never looked bluer. I didn't even notice it at the time, but I tore my fingernails down until they were bleeding, trying to make a hole in the runway, I guess. Across the runway, I found a hole about 4 feet deep and 10 feet across, which I dove into and, for the first time since the bombing began, I felt like I had made it. I was in the pit, which I learned later was dug for a base perimeter security exercise, for no more than five minutes when one of our large refueling trucks pulled up and stopped with one of his tires flat from being hit by one of the strafers. I could just picture another strafer hitting the truck and filling my hole with flaming fuel. I jumped from my security blanket and was out in the open again.

Finally, the driver of the truck, who was a kid from my squadron, and I decided things were quieting down. He went back to the motor pool and had them bring out a huge jack and for at least the next hour, I helped him change the wheel. I then went back across the runway to the 5th Bomber Group Personnel Office where a bunch of guys I knew had gathered. When Mike Kocan saw me, he said that he went by my quarters earlier and thought I had been killed. He told me that a small bomb hit up against the curb in front of my house and blew right through it. When I finally got back to my house (Tuesday PM) I found that my wristwatch, knocked from the top of my dresser into the open drawer, had the only piece of glass in the house that wasn't broken, including the tiles in the bathroom.

Aboard the USS *Pennsylvania* (in dry dock)
Art Wells—U.S. Marine, Private First Class
19 years old

The huge red ball blossoming under the plane's wing filled the porthole on USS *Pennsylvania,* as the fighter banked and climbed for altitude. The plane had just completed a strafing run on Ford Island, located in the middle of Pearl Harbor. I didn't need for anyone to remind me that it was an unfriendly, because I recognized it as a Jap Zero.

I had just dropped the daily report off and stopped for a bull session with a deck division friend when the sound of explosions reverberated through the ship. We laughed at a nearby sailor's remark, "That's just like the Army to wait until Sunday to hold gunnery practice." But we rushed to a porthole when another sailor yelled, "The Japs are attacking!"

The pace had been leisurely on the ships in Pearl Harbor, the 7th of December 1941, because Sunday was the day for rest and relaxation after the usual weekly few days at sea where the crews practiced day and night for war. Some men were still ashore; some of those aboard were still feeling the effects of a night out in Honolulu; and others were writing letters, pressing uniforms, shining shoes, straightening wall-locker gear, or rapping in bull sessions. With the surprise and suddenness of the attack some would die with a shoe still in hand, or with thoughts of how to word the next sentence in a letter, or with mouths open as they began the next sea story—their war had ended before it had officially begun!

I turned from the porthole and raced aft, heading for my battle station high on the mainmast—I was the pointer on the director controlling the port 5-inch .51-caliber broadside guns. As I dodged others racing to their stations, the expressions on faces registered shocked disbelief, anger, and determination, and some had fear stamped indelibly into their pale and drawn features. . . .

Though Marines usually didn't take their rifles to shipboard battle stations, I instinctively thought of my "best friend." As I sped through the Marine Compartment, I noticed Sgt. Bud Tinker standing near the weapons locker and I slowed to ask whether I could get my rifle. He didn't have a key so I resumed my sprint aft.

I had to climb a ladder up the outside of the most starboard leg of the mainmast's tripod to get to my battle station. Countless times up and down it in practice had given me the agility and confidence of a monkey. . . .

After reaching my station, I helped the men already there lower the storm windows into recesses. I uncovered the gun director, donned a sound-power phone headset, and made checks with the captains of the five-port-side broadside guns. The 5-inch .51-caliber guns were not designed for use against aircraft so the director and gun crews could do nothing but watch harbor activities. . . .

As a 19-year old, I didn't want to miss anything and my eyes darted about the harbor trying to keep tabs on every Jap plane, every bomb and torpedo, and every ship. My attention switched back and forth from Ford Island to Battleship Row, and to *Helena* and *Oglala* berthed in the *Pennsylvania's* regular 10–10 Dock berth, with *Oglala* outboard of *Helena*.

Battleship Row was across the channel and I had an unobstructed and relatively close-up view of it by looking across *Pennsylvania's* starboard quarter. I didn't think of the dangers caused by strafing Jap planes, or of low-level American small-caliber fire, or of a 5-inch AA gun's projectile hitting the mast when it was fired at low-flying planes. I was so engrossed in watching events across the channel that I didn't notice when three planes strafed *Pennsylvania's* port side at about 0805.

The gun director crews were supposed to huddle between the tripod's legs running up through the station during strafing attacks but I leaned out a window for a better view of low-flying planes or flights passing over at higher altitude. Twice, Lieutenant Rogers grasped my belt and pulled me inboard. Even though he reminded me to stay between the legs, I would become engrossed in following the action and ease back to an opening.

With the ship shuddering from the constant concussions caused by the firing of her 5- and 3-inch guns, and the explosions of bombs and torpedoes in the harbor, I didn't consciously feel, hear, or see the gigantic explosion that demolished *Arizona*. Only minutes after the attack had begun, the dreadnought turned into a mass of twisted, torn, and fire-scorched steel.

I didn't pay much attention to activities around *California,* or the tanker *Neosho* directly across the harbor, or

Ford Island. My concentration focused on *Oklahoma* and *West Virginia* as torpedoes ripped again and again into their bowels.

Oklahoma's masts appeared to be moving closer and I realized she was listing heavily to port. Then I watched in awe as she continued turning—so fast her masts splashed the water—until her keel was exposed to the dimmed light of a smoke-shielded sun. When she rolled I could see men spilling off her decks into the water to port and others frantically scrambling over her hull to starboard.

I was in a quandary as I debated with myself whether I should salute. To me the ship was dying in shame and I didn't feel she rated a salute, but I wanted to pay respects to the many men who were dying with her. By the time I'd firmed my decision, she had capsized so I snapped a quick, but reverent, salute.

As *Oklahoma* rolled, a float-equipped scout plane slid off the aft-turret catapult and floated into the burning oil at the channel side of the ship. My attention switched to *West Virginia* and other activities so I didn't watch the plane's final fate but it must have burned and sunk.

I watched while torpedo planes continued attacking *West Virginia*. In what seemed only a matter of seconds after a plane dropped a torpedo, a plume of water spouted at the outboard side of the ship . . . she appeared to rise, shudder, and then settle back even lower in the water than she had been before as the explosions tore out her bowels.

How could anything possibly penetrate a battleship's thick armor I had wondered . . . that it could be done was being demonstrated to me in a most dramatic and definite way!

The Jap planes were below my height when they dropped low to lay their deadly cargoes into the water, as they made torpedo runs on *Helena* and *Oglala*. I could see the cockpit instruments and the expressions on the pilots' faces. The white of their teeth flashed as they grimaced with concentration or grinned in exultation at the success of their missions. Then as the planes banked and climbed for altitude, I was almost eyeball-to-eyeball with the rear gunners as they looked down their gun sights and sprayed deadly bullets over the topsides of the ships. How I wished for my rifle!

My eyes focused on a plane struggling to gain altitude after attacking Ford Island. Flames and smoke streamed out behind it. Then it slipped off to the left and glided to a crash on or near the Navy yard hospital grounds—it was the only plane I saw shot down during the attack!

Approximately 30 minutes after the attack began, orders were passed for the director crew to clear the mainmast and go below. I dropped down the tripod leg ladder, grasping the handrails loosely and tightening my grip occasionally to control my speedy descent . . . my feet were catching every third or fourth rung! I ran to the boat deck and joined a line of sailors and Marines passing ammunition to a 5-inch .25-caliber AA gun—I felt better now that I was helping to fight Japs.

CHAPTER 11

THE JAPANESE ADMIRAL
HEADS FOR HOME

ADMIRAL NAGUMO WAS VERY NERVOUS. AS he and Admiral Kusaka and the others of the staff stood on the flag bridge of the *Akagi* and watched the black dots that were the returning aircraft of the first strike, Nagumo's basic emotion was not elation that he had won a signal victory, but relief that he had not lost any carriers and very few aircraft.

From the outset, Nagumo had opposed the Pearl Harbor attack as too dangerous, and he had not lost his fear. Now his fears of failure were compounded by the worsening of the weather. The returning planes were flying into high seas and tricky winds that would make landings difficult. It was just another worry, added to the many that troubled Admiral Nagumo.

As Commander Fuchida's plane returned toward the carriers, he was already thinking of the third strike they should launch that afternoon. He had looked over the submarine base, which was undamaged, and the fuel tank area, where the Americans kept the oil and gasoline that had to be shipped into Hawaii from the American mainland. He had looked over the dry docks and repair facilities, and it had occurred to him that the capabilities of Pearl Harbor as a naval base had not been touched, although the fleet had been hit and the airfields blasted. But he also knew that it would not take much time to repair the runways and to replace the aircraft of the air forces. If the ship facilities and the fuel supplies were destroyed, a really hard blow would have been struck against the Americans, and they would not be able to use Pearl Harbor as a naval base for many months.

There was no question in Commander Fuchida's mind, then, but that another air strike or perhaps two were in order to finish the job well begun that morning.

As the flying officers came in to the deck of the flagship *Akagi,* they reported to Air Officer Masuda for debriefing.

The air officer had set up a blackboard on the flight deck near the bridge structure. As each officer reported, he was questioned and his story of the damage was entered on the blackboard. Commander Genda came down to the flight deck a few times, eager for the final results as seen by the fliers. The second time he came down, quite a number of the pilots were on hand, and they pressed him to stage another attack. He was noncommittal.

At this time, another meeting of quite a different nature was in progress, at the White House in Washington. There, President Roosevelt had gathered together Secretary of War Stimson, Secretary of the Navy Knox, Secretary of State Hull, Chief of Naval Operations Stark, and Army Chief of Staff Marshall for a war conference, the first they held in World War II. President Roosevelt was issuing a barrage of orders, grounding private aircraft, renewing guard for military installations, and rounding up Japanese and German aliens.

The President knew that the results of Pearl Harbor were tragic, but in another sense they were welcome to him. For months he had labored under the shadow of American isolationism, trying to strengthen American defenses and assist the British in the war effort he knew was essential to control the march of fascism. Now, for the first time, his enemies had served him well, silencing once and for all the isolationists who had claimed that Roosevelt was leading them to a war that no one wanted. Now the war had been forced on America by the Japanese.

Roosevelt that afternoon decided that he would ask Congress next day for a Declaration of War against Japan. Soon he was on the transatlantic telephone conferring with Prime Minister Winston Churchill, learning of the Japanese attack on northern Malaya that same day, and agreeing that they would both make declarations of war against Japan.

It was four o'clock in the morning in Manila when the word of the Pearl Harbor attack began to seep through the naval and army commands. Admiral Thomas Hart, Commander-in-Chief of the Asiatic Fleet, had been awakened from sound sleep to hear the news. General Douglas MacArthur, Commander of U.S. Forces in the Far East, had also learned, and within the first hour he had a telephone call from the army war plans office in Washington, warning him that he should expect an attack at any time.

At 4:00 A.M. the air commander in the Philippines, Lt. General Lewis H. Brereton, put his aircrews on standby alert and asked permission to send his B-17s on a preemptive strike against the Japanese Formosa airfields. Had this been done, the Japanese planes would have been caught on the ground, but MacArthur refused to allow Brereton to act. Seven hours later that failure brought about total disaster to the air force in the Philippines, when the Japanese naval air force struck in great strength and caught the B-17s on the ground.

Commander Fuchida started back for the flagship *Akagi* with photographs of the damage done at Pearl Harbor. He counted four battleships sunk and three badly damaged. The airfields, he noted, had been efficiently destroyed as operational bases for the present.

It was nearly noon when the messenger carrying the war warning from General Marshall arrived at Fort Shafter with the message, and it was a long time before it was finally decoded. By that time it was not only useless, it was a grim reminder that Washington had not done its job and the army and navy commands at Pearl Harbor were the victims.

Commander Fuchida's plane was the last to board the

Akagi that day and did not arrive until almost noon. He immediately rushed to the bridge of the carrier to report to Admiral Nagumo. Instead of pleased congratulations he faced two questions from the worried Nagumo: Was the American fleet badly enough damaged that it would be out of operation for six months? Where were the American carriers?

Commander Fuchida said that he felt the damage to the fleet had been adequate to keep it out of action for six months, but that he had no idea where the American carriers were located. He brushed by the question. The thing to do now, he said enthusiastically, was to launch another strike and smash the Americans' oil storage and dockyard facilities. That way they would know that even if the carriers came back the fleet would not be able to operate out of Hawaii for a long time.

He and Genda had ordered the planes to be refueled and rearmed and ready for departure on another mission. Fuchida then went to the briefing room, where the pilots were continuing their attack reports.

But on the bridge of *Akagi,* Admiral Nagumo was having many thoughts about the whole situation he faced. He had done what he had been ordered to do, he said, he had attacked Pearl Harbor and protected the navy's flank so the American fleet could not interrupt the southern operations against Malaya and the Dutch East Indies.

He had done all he could do, said Admiral Nagumo.

Commander Genda disagreed. He and Fuchida both urged another air strike to knock out the Pearl Harbor bases definitely.

But where were the American carriers? Asked Admiral Nagumo, again. What if they came swooping down on him now, when his planes were off on another air strike that might not produce very much? If he stuck around here, he was risking three quarters of the Japanese Combined Fleet's carrier strength to wipe out port facilities. And they could expect higher losses. Only nine planes had failed to return from the first strike, but the second strike had cost twenty planes. A third strike must be even more costly as the American defenses were gotten into shape. Also, Nagumo argued, he was now within range of American land-based air forces, and no one knew what might happen.

He was growing more nervous every minute.

Nagumo's chief of staff, Admiral Kusaka, took the admiral's side. Fuchida came to protest the decision not to attack again and was silenced. One by one the Nagumo staff came around to the side of their admiral. Instead of the council of victory that had been expected, the talk on the *Akagi* bridge sounded more like a council of despair. The Nagumo staff and the admiral were now worried about the safety of their carrier force and aircraft, not about inflicting damage on the enemy.

Who could prove that the Americans did not have enough planes left on the land to launch an attack against the carriers?

No one.

And where were the American carriers?

Fuchida and Genda had to admit that the American carriers undoubtedly would now begin looking for the Japanese task force. This fact impressed Nagumo very much, and very negatively. It appealed to all his fears. He asked Genda what he thought of the possibility of an enemy strike against the Japanese force.

Let the enemy come, said Commander Genda. If they did come, then the task force would shoot down their planes. But that sort of argument did not affect Nagumo except to make him ever more fearful. The responsibility was his, not theirs.

Fuchida left the bridge, disgusted and heartsick at the timidity. Genda took over the argument. He was not satisfied with the damage done, he warned. Japan had the chance of a lifetime to damage the Pacific Fleet if they would only stay and finish the job. Genda did not advocate another attack that day. The aircraft had already been rearmed to meet an attack from ships at sea, in case the enemy carriers showed up. Let it remain that way. Let them wait, and let them find the American carriers. Let them stay in the area for two or three days to see what happened, and run down the enemy carriers as they appeared.

Nagumo considered the course. It went against all he believed, for his basic emotion was fear that he would overreach his capability and sacrifice one or more of the carriers—needlessly as it now seemed, since he had already achieved a victory over the American fleet that his officers said would be out of action for six months.

What Genda now wanted was for Nagumo to send out scout planes and find the American carriers, while bringing down the tankers from the north and refueling and preparing for more action. What should be done now was to find the American carriers and destroy them, one by one, then go back and hit Pearl Harbor again on the way to the Marshall Islands. Hit Pearl Harbor hard, destroy the fuel and repair facilities, and return to Japanese waters knowing that they had pulled the teeth of the enemy fleet.

In the face of the younger officers' hopes for a total victory, which they saw as achieved in one or two days of continued action, was the almost united view of the Nagumo staff, which wanted to play it safe and go home with what they had.

When this word came to Admiral Ugaki, Admiral Yamamoto's chief of staff, he characterized Nagumo as like the thief in the henhouse, who takes fright and runs off with a chicken or two when he could have the whole coop. He asked Admiral Yamamoto to order Nagumo to continue the action, but this Yamamoto refused to do. He also felt that Nagumo was chickenhearted, but he respected the right of the officer in command on the scene to make the decisions, no matter how much he disagreed, and he would not interfere with Nagumo.

Nagumo had to make up his mind; no, that was not really true. His mind had been made up from the beginning. He wanted to take the easy way, with the least danger to the striking force. They had achieved a victory beyond the furthest dreams of any but Yamamoto already, and Nagumo and his staff were not willing to go further. Nagumo vacillated, but his staff was strong and steady on the subject. They must return and go home now, said Admiral Kusaka.

He remembered, as did Admiral Nagumo, how much the Naval General Staff had disliked the Yamamoto plan from the beginning. He remembered that the basis on which they had gotten the six carriers instead of the four originally authorized was that they would all be made available immediately after the Pearl Harbor operation for use in the southern waters to support the Malaya and Dutch East Indies operations.

Admiral Nagumo and his staff had already forgotten what Admiral Yamamoto had told them; this was a great gamble and they should be prepared to lose a third of their force if necessary to accomplish the aims. They had accomplished it all so far without a scratch to the ships and a minimal loss of aircraft. Instead of considering the resources he had left and the damage they could inflict on the enemy, Nagumo and his staff were now considering their own safety and determined not to risk the task force at all.

Nagumo and Kusaka said to themselves that they had

achieved 80 percent of what they wanted, and the other 20 percent was not worth the risk. But Genda and Fuchida said that the other 20 percent was the difference between success and basic failure. Nagumo could not see that in any sense he was failing by refusing to finish the job. So he persisted in his desire to leave the scene, his staff backed him, and the aviators, Genda and Fuchida and the flight leaders, were overwhelmed by the determined timidity of their superiors.

Kusaka was very pleased. He had opposed the whole operation from the beginning, but he had given his word to Yamamoto once the orders were given that they would be obeyed and the strike would be carried out. Now it had been carried out, and what was wanted by others was more than the call of duty, a risk to win a real victory rather than a partial one, and Kusaka was not interested. He wanted to get the carriers back to Japan, where they could join in what he saw as the primary operation, the drive south.

And the admirals had their way.

The airmen asked Genda for an explanation of what they saw as a wrongheaded decision; Genda gave them three reasons:

1. The attack had achieved its expected results.
2. A second attack would bring new risks to the task force.
3. They did not know where the American carriers were.

Commander Genda dutifully made the excuses for Admiral Nagumo, but privately he called Nagumo a "miscast misfit" and lamented the fact that they had not been given either Admiral Ohnishi or Admiral Yamaguchi, both aggressive airmen, to command the operation. It was all the fault of the naval ministry, said the young officers, for putting this power into the hands of a man who was basically a "battleship admiral," and who did not understand the basics of carrier warfare.

And so that afternoon, as the carriers were being made read for another attack, the order came down from the Nagumo bridge. "Preparations for attack canceled," said the signal flags, and they were followed by others that announced the flagship's intention to retire to the northwest.

Commander Fuchida was just grabbing a bit of late lunch when he learned all this. He rushed to the bridge, saluted Admiral Nagumo, and asked, "Why aren't we attacking again?"

Nagumo opened his mouth, but Admiral Kusaka answered, "The objectives of the Pearl Harbor attack have been achieved. Now we must prepare for other operations ahead."

Fuchida saluted and turned on his heel, unable to speak for frustration and anger.

And so the striking force began to retire. Still this was not quite the end of the story. . . .

CHAPTER 12

DECLARATION OF WAR

IN HONOLULU, JUST A FEW MILES FROM Pearl Harbor, the initial Japanese attack created no stir at all. The people of the city were used to strange doings at Pearl Harbor and on the west side of the island, where the navy and the army conducted training and maneuvers. It was not until nine o'clock that morning, when the first attack was nearly spent, that radio station KGMB broadcast the news that the Japanese had attacked. "This is the real McCoy," said the announcer. And then people began to believe that the rumors they had been hearing were true.

At the Japanese consulate, the early arrivals milled about, not knowing what to believe. Only when a reporter from the *Honolulu Star Bulletin* arrived with a copy of the Extra announcing

WAR! OAHU BOMBED BY JAPANESE PLANES

did the consulate staff realize that the attack was in progress, and then the staff began burning papers. In midmorning, the FBI arrived and carted off many documents for the intelligence office at fleet headquarters.

President Roosevelt had just finished lunch in the Oval Office when Secretary Knox telephoned and told him about the Pearl Harbor attack. The Japanese ambassadors had not yet delivered their final message breaking off peace discussions to Secretary Hull, and Hull was not sure whether or not he should receive them under the circumstances. Roosevelt told him to receive them, but to say nothing about Pearl Harbor.

So when Admiral Nomura and Ambassador Kurusu, the Japanese diplomats, gave Hull their final message, the Secretary of State received them coldly, commented on the nature of their message, which he termed a pack of lies, and dismissed them. Admiral Nomura did not then know that the Japanese Navy had already attacked Pearl Harbor and did not find out until he returned to his home later in the afternoon. He was profoundly shocked, particularly at the position into which he had been put by his government.

Secretary of War Stimson was having a late lunch when he learned the news. He had a feeling of relief that the crisis had come, and in a way that it would unite Americans. In spite of the fact that the Pearl Harbor strike was a catastrophe, he welcomed its implications, for it put an end to the bickering about a war that he found inevitable.

Army Chief of Staff Marshall was having lunch when the news came. He hurried back to his office, where he remained until 3:00 P.M. when he had an appointment with President Roosevelt.

Secretary Hull stayed at the State Department until 3:00 P.M. and then went to the White House to join General Marshall and the President and several other advisers. Admiral Stark stayed at the navy department and kept relaying the bad news from Hawaii to the White House by telephone.

President Roosevelt telephoned Governor Poindexter in Hawaii and was talking to him when Poindexter suddenly announced that the second wave of bombers had just appeared and was working over Oahu.

President Roosevelt and General Marshall discussed the Philippines, and Marshall told the President that he had warned General MacArthur and MacArthur could be expected to take the necessary precautions against surprise in the Philippines.

The White House meeting broke up shortly and the various advisers went their own ways. Secretary Hull went back to the State Department, where he presided over a meeting of his own.

On the street in front of the White House and around Lafayette Park, several hundred people gathered to show their anger and frustration over the Japanese attack. They continued to come and go all afternoon and evening, with police urging them to disperse, but gently.

At around eleven o'clock that morning, Hawaii time, the destroyer *Ward* had used up all her depth charges, bombing what appeared to be many submarine contacts. Just after that, with the *Monaghan* and other destroyers now outside and sharing the work load, Lieutenant Outerbridge took the *Ward* inside the harbor, went to the ammunition depot, and renewed the supplies of depth charges. This time Lieutenant Outerbridge took aboard all the depth charges the ship could carry. By three o'clock that afternoon they were back outside, searching again for enemy submarines. They continued all day and evening to make contacts.

The afternoon of December 7, 1941, Admiral Kimmel and his staff were awaiting another strike by the Japanese when they had word of the first Japanese action against Guam, an air raid by planes from Saipan, which sank the naval ship *Penguin* in Apia Harbor. Shortly afterward came the word that Wake Island had been hit by the Japanese too, and seven of the new fighters delivered by Admiral Halsey had been destroyed. The Pan American Clipper, which had stopped over at Wake, had escaped and was on its way to Midway. The pilot radioed that he saw a Japanese cruiser and several destroyers that were heading for Wake. So it was apparent that the Japanese attack in the Pacific was general, and that worse news could be expected.

It was not long in coming. The news of heavy air raids on Hong Kong and the bombing of Singapore came next. From Shanghai came the word that the gunboat *Wake* had been captured. Then came word of two bombing attacks on the Philippines, and still MacArthur would not loosen the hands of his air commander to make retaliatory strikes. By late afternoon, the question in the Philippines was moot, for the Japanese had come to the

Clark Field complex and had virtually wiped out American air power in their air raids.

It was mid-afternoon by the time that Commander Layton was able to tell Admiral Kimmel that the Japanese attackers had come from the north. The information came from the pilot's compartment of a downed Japanese plane. The pilot's plot board had been saved, and it showed the plane's course from the carrier force more than two hundred miles north of Oahu, and the course he should fly to get back, if he had been so lucky as to make it. But by this time the Japanese task force was already moving back out of range of American carriers.

Kimmel's orders to Task Force 8 were to search for the enemy. One of the Japanese submarines intercepted the message and warned Admiral Nagumo that the enemy was searching for him. But they were not looking in the north; they were looking to the south. One of the pilots of the B-17s remembered that he had seen Japanese planes coming from the north that morning, and he tried to interest people at air force headquarters in that information. But no one listened. "They seemed more interested in fitting liners inside helmets," the pilot remarked.

At about 1:00 P.M., Hawaii time, the Japanese striking

force turned back north at 26 knots. Admiral Nagumo was worried again that the American carriers would find his force. At just after five o'clock that evening Nagumo ordered the ships to battle stations, and set up a combat air patrol that would go out at dawn 360 degrees in full circle and travel out to 300 miles around the carrier force.

That night the Japanese force made itself ready in case of discovery of the American carriers. Commander Genda prepared the bombers for torpedoing and dive-bombing the next day. Commander Fuchida told all officers to develop their attack photos for study of damage done to the American fleet. Planes from the other five carriers brought all their photos to the flagship, where the air intelligence officers studied them half the night. On the morning of December 8, Nagumo sent the light cruiser *Chikuma* and a destroyer to meet the supply group at the rendezvous point. The ships refueled and then brought the tankers down to join the fleet.

On December 8th in Tokyo, Imperial General Headquarters proclaimed that a state of war existed between Japan and the United States and British Empire.

In Washington, on the evening of December 7, all the members of the Roosevelt cabinet assembled in the

White House Oval Office. President Roosevelt gave his cabinet members a summary of the events of the day and drew a parallel with the cabinet meeting of President Lincoln on the eve of the Civil War.

That night Secretary Stimson suggested that the President also declare war on Germany the next day when he spoke to Congress, but Roosevelt refused. He said that this would play into the hands of the isolationists. And besides, he knew from intercepts of Japanese coded messages that Foreign Minister von Ribbentrop had promised the Japanese ambassador to Berlin that Germany would declare war on the United States.

President Roosevelt made a point of inviting the Democratic and Republican leaders of Congress to this meeting, and they came in a little later. Roosevelt again catalogued the day's events.

The Congressional leaders tended to be caustic in the extreme. Senator Tom Connally charged that the army and the navy had been asleep at the switch, and he harried Secretary Knox because the navy did not "do anything" to the enemy that made the attack. Why were the ships all crowded together in Pearl Harbor, he wanted to know. Had not Secretary Knox just two weeks earlier said that America could defeat the Japanese navy in two weeks? Where were the American patrols, that they let the Japanese through to attack?

Finally the Congressional delegation left, still with many questions in the minds of the members, and much dissatisfaction with the conduct of the administration. But when they left, they agreed on one thing: From this day it would not be politics as usual. Senator McNary and other Republican leaders promised that whatever President Roosevelt did in this crisis, the country would be solidly behind him.

Later, that night, President Roosevelt had his latest shock, the news, that in spite of all the warnings, General MacArthur had allowed himself to be surprised in the Philippines and that most of the American air force there had been wiped out in the day's Japanese air raids.

Next morning, Monday, the fire fighters at Pearl Harbor were still working to put out the blazes started by the Japanese attack. Rescue parties were still working among the battleships, trying to rescue men trapped inside the steel hulls. One by one the sounds of tapping stopped, the air supplies ran out, and the men inside the steel hulls suffocated or drowned.

That Monday morning, Admiral Kimmel assembled his staff of the Pacific Fleet to discuss the offensive measures he wanted to undertake. On balance, the disaster at Pearl Harbor had not seemed quite so disastrous. Kimmel had the two task forces, *Enterprise* and *Lexington,* at hand, and they could be sent out immediately. The carrier *Saratoga* was moving toward Pearl Harbor at that moment from the West Coast, to add to the offensive strength of the fleet. Kimmel also had nine heavy cruisers, all but two of the fleet's light cruisers, and all but three of the fleet's destroyers with which to work.

That morning, Admiral Wilson Brown's Task Force 12, built around the *Lexington,* was chasing after a rumor that the Japanese had attacked Johnston Island, but that rumor was dispelled by afternoon. North of Oahu, Rear Admiral Milo F. Draemel's light cruisers and the heavy cruiser *Minneapolis* were chasing the Japanese, fruitlessly as it turned out. Southwest of Oahu, Admiral Halsey was still looking for the Japanese, which Captain McMorris thought were down there, but that evening Task Force 8 came into Pearl Harbor, refueled, and then went out again. This time, Halsey caught a fish: the Japanese submarine *I-70,* which the task force sank with a great deal of satisfaction.

On December 8, President Roosevelt spoke to a joint

session of Congress in the House of Representatives, where he characterized the events of December 7:

Yesterday, December 7, 1941—a date which will live in infamy—the United States was suddenly and deliberately attacked by the naval and air forces of the Empire of Japan. . . .

Congress passed the war resolution then, with a single dissenting vote.

AFTERWORD

DESPITE WEEKS AND EVEN MONTHS OF warnings, the attack on Pearl Harbor was a severe shock to the military and government leaders in Washington. It was also a shock to the ordinary people of the United States. This shock quickly turned to resolve and soon the country was firmly united in the cause of turning back the threats to the world from both Japan and Germany. Soon the enormous power of the economy in the United States was aimed squarely at building the ships, airplanes, tanks, guns, and ammunition necessary for the task. As Admiral Yamamoto had warned, Japan had awakened a sleeping giant and the giant would not rest until the job was finished.

The day after the attacks at Pearl Harbor recruiting

offices for the Army, Navy, and Marines were crowded with young men wanting to join up. Not only were soldiers and sailors asked to do their part, but everyone in the country joined in the effort as well. Women who had never worked outside their homes signed up to work in factories building everything necessary for the war effort. Children collected scrap tin cans and aluminum foil that would be made into jeeps, bullets, and airplane wings. All the lights in houses, stores, and along roads near both the Atlantic and Pacific coasts were blacked out at night to prevent enemy submarines from identifying potential targets. Many things were rationed in the United States including food and gasoline so that the troops could be properly supplied. Few complained. Everyone felt it was important to make sacrifices to win the war. The attack on Pearl Harbor had galvanized the country.

As for the damage inflicted on Pearl Harbor, many of the damaged battleships were repaired and sent back to sea within a year. However, almost immediately navy leaders realized how lucky it was that their aircraft carriers had been spared at Pearl Harbor. The attack on Pearl Harbor had taught them that war at sea had changed and that carriers had become the most important ships in the navy. That would soon be demonstrated in a great battle at sea that would take place near the tiny island of Midway only six months later.

THE EDITORS

Index

ABOUT THE AUTHOR

EDWIN P. HOYT served in the Pacific theater during World War II and afterward became a war correspondent in Asia and the Middle East. He was a news editor for the U.S. Office of War Information and a member of the psychological warfare team in India, Burma, and China. He was a reporter for the *Denver Post* and the *San Francisco Chronicle* as well as a producer for CBS News.

An avid military historian, Hoyt is the author of more than 150 books.